W9-ANN-721

"I've done a lot of interviews, but I would say that these guys stand out the best . . . They took so much time researching my background to help me. If the market goes down, I'm not affected."

—Susan, graphic artist

"I've had bad experiences with the stock market. Now, my financial future is looking much better. We had an instant connection—they're a fun bunch, and it's not always serious, which I appreciate. They're always there if I have a question."

—Hildegarde, hair stylist

"How do I manage the changes in my retirement? What strategies do I need? Well, the company is giving me the answers just in its name. We sat down, and he would show me what my options are, what are the advantages and disadvantages. If I didn't trust them, I wouldn't be dealing with them."

—Lita, retired photographer

"I Just heard on the news about yet another plunge in the stock market, and it is so wonderful to not feel that cold shiver of dread. I'm so glad we met you folks and that we're doing business with you."

—Susan Wade

SECURE RETIREMENT STRATEGIES

FACTS VS. FICTIONS

SECURE RETIREMENT STRATEGIES

FACTS VS. FICTIONS

MARC SMITH & MICHAEL NEFT

Published by Advantage, Charleston, South Carolina.
Member of Advantage Media Group.

ADVANTAGE is a registered trademark, and the Advantage colophon is a trademark of Advantage Media Group, Inc.

Printed in the United States of America.

ISBN: 978-1-59932-748-8
LCCN: 2016938619

This publication is designed to provide accurate and authoritative information in regard to the subject matter covered. It is sold with the understanding that the publisher is not engaged in rendering legal, accounting, or other professional services. If legal advice or other expert assistance is required, the services of a competent professional person should be sought.

Advantage Media Group is proud to be a part of the Tree Neutral® program. Tree Neutral offsets the number of trees consumed in the production and printing of this book by taking proactive steps such as planting trees in direct proportion to the number of trees used to print books. To learn more about Tree Neutral, please visit **www.treeneutral.com.** To learn more about Advantage's commitment to being a responsible steward of the environment, please visit **www.advantagefamily.com/green.**

Advantage Media Group is a publisher of business, self-improvement, and professional development books and online learning. We help entrepreneurs, business leaders, and professionals share their Stories, Passion, and Knowledge to help others Learn & Grow. Do you have a manuscript or book idea that you would like us to consider for publishing? Please visit **advantagefamily.com** or call **1.866.775.1696.**

To our wives, Susan Smith and Lois Neft, for their support, help, and understanding during the writing of this book.

And to all the retirees we have helped and those we will help in the future.

CONTENTS

ABOUT THE AUTHORS

Marc Smith is a managing partner at Secure Retirement Strategies, where he draws on his twenty-five years of financial services experience to help retirees and near-retirees meet their retirement needs. By listening to his clients and drawing on his diverse product knowledge, Marc ensures that his clients get the custom-designed retirement plan that's right for them.

Before joining Secure Retirement Strategies, Marc was a managing partner of a leading financial organization, where he initiated the unique Suite of Services platform. This service brought to the marketplace the broadest range of nonproprietary products together under one roof.

Some of Marc's other career highlights include being recognized for the past fifteen years with the prestigious GAMA Master Agency Award; the GAMA International Management Diamond Award in 2012; youngest partner and leading sales manager in the United States at New York Life; Top of the Table qualification in his fourth year in the business; and number-two ranking in his second year in the business with Equitable Life Insurance Company.

Marc is regarded for his honesty, passion, integrity, relationship building, and high ethical standards; he is a certified member of the National Ethics Association, and he is involved in many charitable organizations. While Marc is pleased with all he has accomplished, his achievements pale in comparison to the pleasure he gains from helping others. When he's not working, he enjoys travel, exercise, art, reading, and spending time with his wife and four sons.

To contact Marc:
Phone: 610.888.4673
E-mail: msmith@srsstrategies.com

Michael Neft is a managing partner at Secure Retirement Strategies, where he relies on nearly forty years of experience in finance and securities. He is always looking for new ways to help retirees and near-retirees throughout the country earn income for life as they approach or enter retirement.

Michael has held senior-management positions at heavyweight institutions such as Janney Montgomery Scott, Prudential Securities, and Shearson American Express. Before joining Secure Retirement Strategies, Michael spent seven years as an executive director with Oppenheimer.

Over the course of his career, Michael has attained a special compliance background, with more than twenty years of experience as a dispute-resolution arbitrator for the Financial Industry Regulatory Authority (FINRA). During his tenure with FINRA, Michael has arbitrated more than fifty cases, resolving disputes between brokerage firms, clients and brokerage firms, and employees and brokerage firms. Michael's other affiliations include being a board member of the New York Stock Exchange Disciplinary Hearing Board for eight years, a board member of the New York Stock Exchange Acceptability Board for five years, a member of the National Ethics Association, and a dispute-resolution arbitrator for fourteen years with the National Futures Exchange.

Michael's problem-solving skills were recognized when he was appointed an arbitrator for the National Association of Securities Dealers (NASD) in 1991, the New York Stock Exchange in 1992, and the National Futures Exchange in 2003. In addition, Michael is a Registered Advisor under the NFL Players' Association Financial Advisors Program, a stringent qualifying program sponsored by the NFL Players Union. Michael also holds numerous securities and commodities licenses.

Michael has been married for more than forty years, and he has three sons and a granddaughter. His hobbies include sports, weight training, biking, cooking, travel, and researching and building Napoleonic-era model ships.

To contact Michael:
Phone: 610.639.8976
E-mail: mneft@srsstrategies.com

INTRODUCTION

Are you thinking about retirement? If you're not, you probably should be! The years go by, one after another, and no matter how close or far away it seems now, one day you will face the moment when you retire from your job. You'll be ready to enter the next phase of your life.

But will you *really* be ready? You won't be if you haven't already made a wise financial plan. That's why we wrote this book. We want to help you be ready for retirement.

Together, we have more than fifty years of experience in financial services. We've held senior-management positions at various large financial institutions, and today we are managing partners at Secure Retirement Strategies. We take pride in all that we've accomplished over the years, but we are even prouder of the many individuals we've helped to achieve secure retirements.

In this book, we'll draw on our experiences working with retirees and near-retirees. We've made a habit of listening to our clients, and we've learned a lot from them about how to ensure that each individual has a custom-designed retirement plan. We have a broad knowledge base from which to build, but we're also creative problem solvers who can think outside the box. We're committed to sharing all our skills and experience with our clients—and now with you, as you read this book.

We understand that the very thought of retirement planning can be overwhelming. It doesn't need to be. There are actions you can take now that will prepare you for the future, and we're going to tell you what those are. We'll help you cut through all the fiction that's floating around out there about retirement planning.

And then we'll give you the facts.

CHAPTER 1

I magine you wake up one morning with your tooth throbbing. You get up and go about your day, but by evening, the pain is worse. "What's wrong with me?" you ask yourself. You decide to go online to research your symptoms, and after reading several websites, you're confident you have the answer: the root of your tooth is infected. The abscess is pressing on the nerve, and that's what is causing you so much pain. "All right," you think, "now I know what's wrong, I'll try to put the pain out of my mind." You decide to simply hope for the best. "Maybe the abscess will take care of itself," you tell yourself. "After all, things usually work out in the end. No point in worrying about it."

3

As the days go by, however, the pain grows even worse. Your jaw is swollen. You can't eat, because it hurts too much. You've taken ibuprofen, but the pain's still there. You're getting desperate. Finally, you decide to go online once more to do some more research. Again, you read several websites, and then you nod your head. "Aha!" you say. "I need a root canal."

You continue reading online, but you soon realize that the websites aren't giving you enough information. Now you need something more detailed. You go to the bookstore and buy a book on dental surgery. Back home again, you carefully read through the chapter on root canals. You go out to the garage where you keep your tools, and you get a drill and the smallest drill bit you can find.

"I can do this," you tell yourself. "I'm an intelligent person, and I know how to follow instructions." You read through pages in the book one more time. "I've got it," you assure yourself. "I know exactly what to do."

You turn on the drill, take a deep breath, and open your mouth.

THE HELP YOU NEED

In real life, of course, you would never be this stupid! You would never, ever try to give yourself a root canal. When you have a toothache, you go see your dentist, who has years of training and experience doing root canals.

But when it comes to retirement planning, lots of people think they can wing it without an expert's help. At first, they usually put the whole idea out of their minds. After all, retirement is a long way away, and there are plenty of other things in life that seem far more urgent. As the years go by, though, most people gradually become aware that they will have to think about making a retirement plan.

So they go online and read a little. Maybe they buy a book or two on retirement planning. They're positive there's no need for them to consult an expert. They can figure things out on their own. But really? That makes about as much sense as giving yourself a root canal. When it comes right down to it, you probably don't know nearly enough to plan wisely for your retirement.

There's no reason to feel embarrassed about it. We know you're smart. You've been trained in your job, and you have years of experience in what you do. In fact, you're an expert at it. But odds are good you *weren't* trained as a financial planner. We were, however, so we're going to give you some tips.

Keep in mind that's all we can do in a book like this. No book can give you the individualized plan you need for the years ahead. All we can do here is give you some basic information. We'll show you what the situation is. It's up to you to take it to the next step by sitting down with a flesh-and-blood expert in the field, someone who can work with you one-on-one. (Feel free to give us a call!)

YOU'RE NOT ALONE

Retirement planning is one of those things that are easy to postpone. You may have a nagging little feeling that you should make a plan, but unlike a toothache, your future doesn't seem as urgent as it really is.

There are a lot of Americans who feel the same way. In fact, a 2015 study of 5,474 Americans who were eighteen or older, which was based on an online survey sponsored by Northwestern Mutual, revealed that a lot of us have put our heads in the sand when it comes to thinking about tomorrow. More than two-thirds of the survey participants considered themselves to be "savers" who were putting away money for the future—but at the same time, more than 50 percent had a level of debt that equaled or exceeded their savings. Since more than half of the people surveyed knew their financial plans needed to be improved, it seems that people are starting to "feel the pain." However, more than a third of the study participants had done *nothing* to plan for their financial futures. Two out of five hadn't talked to anyone (not even friends or family!) about retirement planning.[1]

Meanwhile, a 2015 telephone survey of slightly more than a thousand workers and a thousand retirees found that almost a third of all workers have less than $1,000 in savings, and more than half had less than $25,000. The survey, conducted by the nonprofit Employee Benefit Research Institute (EBRI) and Greenwald and Associates, found that many workers' only plan was to put off retirement by working longer and then, once retired, get another job to bring in income. In fact, though, half of the retirees surveyed had had to leave their jobs earlier than they had planned, and less than a quarter were able to work for pay during their retirement.[2]

WHAT IF YOU ALREADY HAVE A PENSION?

If you have a pension plan through your employer, that's great. You're one of the lucky 50 percent of American workers (a percentage that is growing smaller all the time, something we'll talk more about in chapter 3). But that doesn't mean you can put the whole matter of retirement out of your mind with a sigh of relief! If you were to get a phone call saying you'd won an all-expense-paid trip to Hawaii, wouldn't you look into it a little more before you packed your bags? Wouldn't you

---

1 "Millenials and Money: Part Young Idealists, Part Old Souls," Northwestern Mutual, April 7, 2015, https://www.northwesternmutual.com/news-room/122886.
2 "Retirement Confidence Survey," Employee Benefit Research Institute, https://www.ebri.org/surveys/rcs.

want to find out whether you'd be staying in the Honolulu Hilton or a fleabag, no-name motel outside the city? Another recent survey, this one done by Charles Schwab, found out most employees spend twice as much time researching their next vacation spot as they do learning about their employer's retirement plan.[3]

For some reason, though, people simply don't like to think about retirement planning, even though a 2014 study released by Financial Engines found that people who got professional investment help with their retirement plans earned higher median annual returns than those who tried to go it alone.[4] The Charles Schwab study found that, unfortunately, less than a quarter of the people surveyed had used any professional advice to help them understand their retirement plans. On the other hand, nearly 90 percent of them hired a professional to change the oil in their cars!

Even sophisticated investors need help with their retirement plans. A 2015 John Hancock survey found that about a third of all knowledgeable investors still felt the need for professional help with their financial plans for the future, and nearly two-thirds were smart enough to know that when it came to making financial decisions, they needed expert guidance.[5] If you have an employee pension plan, you need to find out more about it. Get all the facts. Make sure you will get the most bang for your buck. And also, be aware that in today's uncertain financial world, employee pension plans aren't the

---

3 "Schwab Survey Finds Workers Highly Value Their 401(k) but Are More Likely to Get Help Changing Their Oil Than Managing Their Investments," Charles Schwab, August 14, 2014, http://pressroom.aboutschwab.com/press-release/schwab-corporate-retirement-services-news/schwab-survey-finds-workers-highly-value-the.
4 "Financial Engines & Aon Hewitt find 401(k) Participants Who Use Professional Help Are Better Off Than Those Who Do Not," financial engines, May 13, 2014, http://ir.financialengines.com/phoenix.zhtml?c=233599&p=irol-newsArticle&ID=1930183.
5 "Working with a Financial Advisor Doubles Retirement Preparedness: John Hancock Retirement Plan Services Survey," John Hancock, January 21, 2016, http://www.johnhancock.com/about/news_details.php?fn=jan2116-text&yr=2016.

sure thing they once were. More and more pensions are being cut. (We'll tell you more about that later.)

HOW MUCH MONEY WILL YOU NEED TO RETIRE?

When people *do* think about their retirement, many times they neglect to figure out exactly how much money they'll really need. According to another recent EBRI survey, only 42 percent of Americans have actually calculated how much money they'll need to save for retirement. An equal percentage has only guessed at the number, and almost all of them guessed too low.[6] That's a problem. Those people are likely to have used up their retirement savings long before they die and will have to make drastic changes in their lifestyles.

You're going to need more money during retirement than you think. You may have heard about a recent study reported in MarketWatch that said just the opposite—that you'll need *less* than you think—but that's only true if you want to *do* less.[7] If you plan on sitting in a rocking chair, never traveling, never going out to eat, never buying new clothes, never buying nice gifts for your grandchildren (in fact, never doing a whole lot of things), then yes, you'll need less money than you do now.

But why settle for that? Modern medicine means that we not only live longer, but many of us also remain healthy and active longer. You've worked hard all your life. Wouldn't you like to have some fun once you have more time in your life to enjoy all the good things life has to offer?

---

6 "2012 Retirement Confidence Survey," Employee Benefit Research Institute, 2012, https://www.ebri.org/surveys/rcs/2012.

7 Robert Powell, "You may need less retirement income than you think," MarketWatch, December 24, 2015, http://www.marketwatch.com/story/you-may-need-less-retirement-income-than-you-think-2015-11-30.

YOU NEED A MORE PROACTIVE APPROACH

Your retirement plan needs to become a priority in life. Thinking about the future shouldn't be scary. It shouldn't be a depressing activity that robs today of its joy. Instead, making a smart retirement plan is something you do for yourself (and the people you hope will share your future). It's a positive, hope-filled, proactive action that gives you greater control over the years ahead. A good retirement plan will let you live life to its fullest in the years to come. It will allow you to make the transition from earning a paycheck to living off your savings—without having to get by on the "bare minimum."

Living is expensive, though. Even if you have no desire to go on luxury cruises or toodle around in a high-end convertible, the price of pretty much everything will go up in the years ahead. Remember, health-care and prescription costs are rising. Your basic living expenses are constantly on the rise. The price of gasoline for your car goes up and down without logic. Even the price of a cup of coffee has increased dramatically and will probably continue to do so. Every year you live is another year you need more income to be financially confident, enjoy yourself, and take care of your responsibilities.

You'll need a retirement-income strategy that takes this into account, one that will last as long as you do. Think about it: for a man reaching age sixty-five today, the average life expectancy is currently eighty-four years of age, and for a woman reaching sixty-five today, the average life expectancy is nearly eighty-seven![8] With the advance of medical technology and modern medicine, many people will live into their nineties or even past one hundred. That's great news, but at

---

8 "Calculators: Life Expectancy," Social Security Adminstration, https://www.ssa.gov/planners/lifeexpectancy.html.

the same time, the longer you live, the further your nest egg is going to have to stretch.

These are supposed to be your golden years. You don't want to have to downsize your lifestyle or be forced to work when you've finally earned the chance to relax a little. So what can you do? You'll need to put your money somewhere smart, somewhere your investment will grow so that inflation doesn't erode it, dollar by dollar, as the years go by.

We're not going to tell you to risk your hard-earned savings in the stock market. Instead, in this book, we're going to tell you about a retirement-income strategy that provides a reliable rate of return, never loses account value in a down market, can be guaranteed to increase over time, and is, possibly, tax-free. That may sound too good to be true, but remember that our goal in this book is to help you sort the facts from the fiction. We're going to give you all the information we can, but in the end, you can't carry out this strategy all by yourself. You'll need smart professional help. We'll talk more about that in the next chapter.

And don't forget that thinking you can manage your own retirement portfolio is pretty much the same as thinking you can give yourself a root canal!

FACT

You need a trusted advisor to help you

plan for your retirement.

CHAPTER 2

FACT OR FICTION:

THE FINANCIAL ADVISOR WHO HELPED
YOU ACCUMULATE WEALTH
IS THE BEST PERSON TO HELP
YOU PLAN FOR RETIREMENT

C limbing Mount Everest has become a symbol for human achievement. More than four thousand people have successfully climbed the 29,035 feet to its top, and for them, that achievement represented a lifetime pinnacle. Although most of us will never climb Mount Everest, you could say, metaphorically speaking, that we are all climbing a financial mountain throughout our professional careers. Before we retire, each of us is laboring toward the summit that lies ahead.

Once climbers reach the top of Mount Everest, their journey isn't over. No one plans on building a house up there and staying forever. The summit is only the halfway point. Now comes the *really* hard part: they have to come back. Sadly, 85 percent of the people who have died on Mount Everest did so while climbing *down* the mountain. It's not that the journey down is so much more dangerous than the climb up the mountain. Instead, say mountain-climbing experts, many climbers work hard to prepare for the upward journey and forget to focus on what they will need to safely descend.

When you reach your financial mountaintop—the moment when you're ready to retire—you've achieved something huge, something that took you years of hard work. But as high-altitude mountaineer Ed Viesturs knows, it's on the mountain's summit, where climbers are cold and exhausted, that they are most at risk. "Getting to the summit is optional," Viesturs wrote in his memoir. "Getting down is mandatory. A lot of people forget about that."[9] Most of the financial industry forgets that too. It's concerned only with reaching the summit.

Thousands of advisors offer strategies that focus on getting their clients to retirement. Then, once their clients reach that mountain-top, they're on their own. Getting down is mandatory, but a lot of people have to navigate the descent all by themselves. Along the way, they're bound to run into a host of unexpected dangers: increased taxes . . . rising inflation . . . unexpected health costs. The journey down the mountain may also take longer than they expected. When that happens to actual mountaineers, they can run out of food and supplies; when retirees live longer than they had planned, they're likely to run out of money if they haven't adequately prepared ahead of time.

---

9 Ed Viesturs, *No Shortcuts to the Top* (New York: Broadway Books, 2006).

What's even worse, of course, is when advisors not only fail to help their clients make a safe plan for retirement, but they also give them bad advice. This is pretty much like a Sherpa who leads climbers to the peak, gives them a list of instructions that will lead them directly into danger, and then waves goodbye.

YOUR FINANCIAL ADVISOR COULD BE GIVING YOU THE WRONG ADVICE

In fact, your investment advisor may not be concerned with your best interests. The problem is so real and so bad that President Obama specifically addressed it back in February 2015. "If you're working hard and saving money," the president said, "sacrificing that new car or vacation so you can build a nest egg for later, you should have the peace of mind that the advice you're getting is sound."[10]

A report released by the Securities and Exchange Commission (SEC) and the Financial Industry Regulatory Authority (FINRA) found that more than a third of brokerage firms are giving bad retirement advice. The most common complaints were poor service and high fees. Instances of misrepresentation, unsuitable investments, churning (pumping up stock sales), and bad advice were all reported.[11]

Here are some of the specific ways that financial advisors sometimes lead their older clients astray:

- *Too much investment in the stock market:* The youngest of the baby boomers will soon be able to start withdrawing from their 401(k)s without penalty, but they may find that

10 President Barack Obama, "Remarks by the President at White House Conference on Aging" (Speech, The White House, July 13, 2015), www.whitehouse.gov/the-press-office/2015/07/13/remarks-president-white-house-conference-aging.
11 Kristin Haugk, "Wall Street Regulations: When the Wolf is Guarding the Henhouse," Wealthy Retirement, November 12, 2015, http://wealthyretirement.com/wolf-is-guarding-the-henhouse-finra-regulatory-notice-15-37.

they're in trouble. At the end of July 2015, when Fidelity Investments released its quarterly analysis of its 401(k)s and IRAs, the data indicated that many boomers have 401(k)s with stock allocations beyond what is recommended, potentially exposing them to excess risk, especially if the market takes a downturn. Eighteen percent of people ages fifty to fifty-four had a stock allocation at least 10 percentage points higher than recommended, and for people ages fifty-five to fifty-nine, that figure increased to 27 percent. Eleven percent of people ages fifty and fifty-four and 10 percent of people ages fifty-five to sixty had their *entire* 401(k) invested in the stock market.[12] Fidelity warned people over fifty that if they want to make their retirement funds last, they need to cut down on stocks. Fidelity's Jim MacDonald stated in an online article:

> One thing we learned from the last recession is that having too much stock, based on your target retirement age, in your retirement account can expose your savings to unnecessary risk—it's the hidden danger that many workers are unaware of. This is especially true among workers nearing retirement, who should be taking steps to protect what they've worked so hard to save.[13]

So why aren't their financial advisors giving them that advice?

---

12 Ibid.
13 "Market Gains Drive Retirement Balances Higher but Too Much Stock Could Put Savings at Risk, Fidelity Analysis Finds," Fidelity, www.fidelity.com/about-fidelity/employer-services/market-gains-drive-retirement-balances-higher.

- *401(k) and IRA rollovers:* Many investment firms tell their clients who are nearing retirement to shift money from their 401(k) into an individualized retirement account (an IRA). In reality, though, there's no good reason to do this. In fact, there's good reason *not* to do it. The 401(k) plans that employers offer often have low fees and good investment choices. The IRA, however, may have fees that are many times as high. So why do financial advisors give their clients this bad advice? Because the advisors get a kickback; it's to their advantage to get clients to open up new and more expensive IRAs.

- *Load fees:* If you buy a mutual fund from a broker, odds are good that you'll be charged what's called a front-load fee. This one-time fee—which helps compensate advisors for their time—can take a hefty gulp out of your money before it's even invested. More and more investors have wised up and are asking for no-load mutual funds, but even so, the Investment Company Institute found that the sale of load funds is increasing, not diminishing. The institute estimated that in 2013, $630 billion in load funds were sold, a 19 percent increase from 2012.[14]

- *Hard-to-see fees:* Load fees are fairly easy to spot, but your advisor may also be getting other commissions you're not aware of. They may be in the fine print somewhere, but the sum of what your advisor is making off your money is never clearly added up for you.

---

14 Ben Steverman, "Five Ways Your Financial Adviser Can Screw Up Your Retirement, Literally," Bloomberg, February 23, 2015, http://www.bloomberg.com/news/articles/2015-02-23/five-ways-your-financial-adviser-can-screw-up-your-retirement-legally.

When you take a look at the fine print, you can see these fees listed:

- omnibus processing fees
- trailers and 12-b fees
- networking fees
- finder's fees
- account-services fees for affiliated fund
- revenue-sharing payments

What those fees actually *mean*, however, is hard to decipher. And there may be still more fees that are undisclosed. (We'll talk more about these fees in later chapters.)

- *A bias for actively managed mutual funds:* A 2012 study sent "investors" to a group of financial advisors to see what sort of advice they'd be given. The advisors told 85 percent of them to get rid of diversified, low-fee portfolios and shift their investments into higher-fee mutual funds that would be actively managed by the advisors.[15] In many investment categories, however, low-fee index funds have a better record than actively managed mutual funds. Other studies conducted a few months earlier (by researchers from Goethe University and the University of Naples)[16] confirmed that accounts that used advisors were more heavily invested in mutual funds and had higher turnovers. Both outcomes earned higher commissions for the advisors

15 Matt Koppenheffer, "The Cold, Hard Truth about Brokers and Financial Advisors," The Motley Fool, March 20, 2012, http://www.fool.com/investing/general/2012/03/20/the-cold-hard-truth-about-brokers-and-financial-a.aspx.
16 Andreas Hackenthal, Michael Halliassos, and Tullio Jappelli, "Financial Advisors: A Case of Babysitters?", Social Science Research Network (SSRN), ssrn.com/abstract=1360440 or http://dx.doi.org/10.2139/ssrn.1360440.

but poorer results for investors. The SEC and FINRA report found that this is particularly a problem for older people planning for retirement or who are already retired. Firms generated the most revenue from seniors by selling open-end mutual funds and variable annuities.

- *Poor-performing investments:* Advisors aren't pushing their clients toward investments that will actually perform well for them. Instead, fees and commissions give advisors selfish incentives to recommend certain investment products over others. Some financial firms also give their advisors additional bonuses when they persuade clients to put their investments into the firms' own funds. The result? Their clients' investment performance suffers. The same study we just mentioned looked at nearly forty thousand random investors who had been offered the option to either manage their accounts or employ an advisor. Folks who had financial advisors had returns that were 5 percent lower (even before fees were deducted) than the accounts that did not. Maybe this doesn't sound like much, but imagine that you start out with a $100,000 portfolio invested with the help of a financial advisor who gets you 7 percent returns instead of the 12 percent returns you might have gotten elsewhere. Over the course of thirty years, that percentage difference will cost you more than $2 million! You'll end up with a portfolio that's worth not quite $800,000 rather than the nearly $3 million you could have had. Why does this happen? Because these financial advisors were focused on padding their own bottom lines rather than their clients' best interests.

Keep in mind that we're not suggesting that you should go it alone as you plan for retirement. Our advice in the previous chapter still stands. What this research does reveal, however, is that you're better off with *no* advice than with bad advice. You're in big trouble if your Sherpa is leading you directly into danger as you descend the mountain!

Meanwhile, the big brokerage houses try hard to convince the public that they put consumers' best interests first. They claim to be fiduciaries, which means they comply with an ethical relationship of trust to take care of their clients' money. A 2015 report issued by the Public Investors Arbitration Bar Association (PIABA), however, cited nine big brokerage houses for advertising as if they were fiduciaries and then, in private arbitration meetings, denying that standard, claiming that they were under no obligation to avoid giving their clients biased advice.[17] The PIABA report's conclusions were based on a 2015 study from the Council of Economic Advisers, which found that investors lose up to $17 billion a year on their independent retirement accounts due to their advisors' conflicts of interest. According to Joe Peiffer, PIABA's president and one of the report's authors, "There's a hypocrisy here, when someone displays one face in public through their statements and advertising, but then they show another face in private."[18]

Think about it like this: If you hire a plumber, you expect to get a plumbing expert who will fix your leaky pipe, not charge you for services he never provides. When you hire a lawyer, she becomes your advocate, representing your best interests—and she doesn't

17 Joseph C. Pfeiffer and Christine Lazaro, *Major Investor Losses Due to Conflicted Advice: Brokerage Industry Advertising Creates the Illusion of a Fiduciary Duty: Misleading Ads Fuel Confusion, Underscore Need for Fiduciary Standard*, Public Investors Arbitration Bar Association report, March 25, 2015, https://piaba.org/system/files/pdfs/PIABA%20Conflicted%20Advice%20Report.pdf.
18 Chuck Jaffe, "Why the Big Broker behind Your Financial Advisor Might Be Working against You," MarketWatch, April 4, 2015.

make deals behind your back that will line her own pockets. So why would you hire a financial advisor who doesn't do the job you need by helping you prepare for your retirement?

The American government knows there's a problem. The 2010 Dodd-Frank Wall Street Reform and Consumer Protection Act was meant to protect investors' interests. It's not working when the big brokerage firms find ways to walk a fine line along the regulations, managing to still promote their own interests over those of their clients. In 2015 President Obama suggested that a fiduciary standard be applied to anyone who works with retirement assets.

Hopefully, change is on its way, but brokerage houses are fighting back. They argue that if all advisors are forced to be fiduciaries, small investors will be unable to get quality advice because their accounts won't generate enough revenues to attract good advisors. That's nonsense. The way things are now, brokerage firms usually give small investors to the less-experienced advisors. In other words, small investors get the equivalent of a Sherpa who's wet behind the ears and still cares most about his own interests rather than the folks he's supposed to be leading safely down the mountainside. Joe Peiffer believes "investors deserve better. Let's hope we get some clarity . . . and that we can eliminate the confusion, because I don't think there's anything worse for an investor than finding out that the person you trusted didn't have your best interests at heart after all."[19]

---

19 Joseph C. Pfeiffer and Christine Lazaro, *Major Investor Losses Due to Conflicted Advice: Brokerage Industry Advertising Creates the Illusion of a Fiduciary Duty: Misleading Ads Fuel Confusion, Underscore Need for Fiduciary Standard.*

WHAT YOU NEED FROM A FINANCIAL ADVISOR

We're not saying that all financial advisors are dishonest crooks. Not by any means. What we *are* saying is that while you may have managed to get to the top of the mountain by accumulating some savings under the guidance of a financial advisor, that same advisor may not have made a plan to get you safely back down the mountain.

Here are some things you should expect from your retirement advisor:

- *Your advisor communicates with you regularly.* In today's uncertain economic climate, you need an advisor who stays in touch with you at all times, especially whenever there's a crisis. Frequent, short communications through e-mail and phone calls are better than long meetings that only take place once or twice a year.

- *Your advisor won't use financial jargon and investment terms that you don't understand.* As Albert Einstein said, "If you can't explain it simply, you don't understand it well enough." Don't be impressed with big words and fancy terms! Insist on clear communications.

- *You can feel free to ask questions and have them answered clearly, respectfully, and thoroughly.* You have a right to know what an advisor is doing with your money and why. Don't be afraid of looking foolish. You may not even know the right questions to ask, but a good advisor will explain his or her reasoning in as much detail you want.

- *You will get a financial plan that's tailor-made for you.* Even if an advisor isn't motivated by self-interest, he may still be too lazy to create a new package for every client who enters his office. Instead, he may have fallen into the habit of dividing his clients into three large groups: conservative risk takers, moderate risk takers, and aggressive risk takers. When he meets with a new client, he assigns her to one of those three categories, and then he dishes out a cookie-cutter portfolio he's created for that group. You need an advisor who will listen to your specific needs and then give you a detailed plan that's built around those needs.

Choosing a financial advisor who will help you prepare for your retirement is serious business. This person is going to be managing the funds and assets that you spent your whole life accumulating. Your advisor's wise counsel could mean the difference between a retirement spent enjoying the things you love and one where you sit at home counting the days until your Social Security check arrives. So take your time when you choose the person who is going to lead you down the mountain!

Here are questions you should always ask your retirement advisor:

- *Are you a fiduciary?* Fiduciaries are obligated to place their clients' financial well-being above their own. At the same time, fiduciaries are held to a higher level of accountability, no pun intended. They are required by law to disclose all their fees and also the ways and amounts by which they are compensated. They must also outline all potential conflicts of interest that could occur in the investing process. You want to make sure you invest with a true fiduciary who will have your best interests in mind and not just see your investment as the means for him to personally make more money.

- *How much do you charge for your services?* Ask for detailed information on how an advisor charges and exactly how he collects on it (directly, through hidden fees, or both).

- *What are your credentials?* Depending on what you want and need out of your investments, this is, potentially, very important information. Ask to see licensing, certification, and any other indicators of past experience and education. There are many people out there claiming the title of financial advisor, but they don't all offer the same level of service. A Certified Financial Planner™ is different from a registered investment advisor, who is required to register with the Securities and Exchange Commission. Chartered Financial Analysts® are another category; they only receive this title after extensive screening from the Certified Financial Advisor's Institute.

- *What services do you specifically provide?* Each financial company provides different potential services. Some financial planners and advisors handle matters of insurance. Others handle estate planning, and some specifically handle retirement. Some handle all three or different elements of each aspect. Be sure to figure this out before investing a dime. Find out if an advisor's specialty is truly retirement, since some organizations will take on retirement funds but specialize in other investments. Be careful.

- *What is your typical investment approach?* An experienced advisor or manager will be able to answer this question quite quickly and skillfully. He will also be able to ask you questions that will allow him to offer examples as to what his strategy would look like for you.

- *Do you understand the level of risk I'm willing to take?* Risk tolerance is an important factor for financial advisors to consider because everyone's level of tolerance is unique. Some financial advisors may take risks with your money with the honest intention of getting you more money, but you may not feel comfortable with that amount of uncertainty. Don't let yourself be pressured into a course of action that doesn't feel right for you.

- *Can you show me a sample financial plan?* With a good sample of a financial plan, an advisor will be able to show you his or her capabilities.

- *How often will you be in contact with me?* Some advisors check in once every quarter, meaning every three months. Others only go over your finances once a year. Make sure you will get the level of communication you want and need.

- *Will you be handling my account alone or working with a team?* Often, two heads (or more) are better than one. This is especially true in the investment world.

- *What sets you apart from your competition?* Every finance and investment firm is different, and it's important that you find out what each offers. What will this advisor do to make your experience unique? You should expect a system that treats each client as an individual, creating personalized plans and solutions.

Bottom line? Don't get stuck at the top of your life's Mount Everest! Make sure your financial guide is able to get you safely through your retirement years.

FACT

Your current financial advisor may not be giving you the advice you need to plan for your retirement.

CHAPTER 3

FACT OR FICTION:
YOUR PENSION FUND WILL
ALWAYS BE THERE

I f you were an eighteenth-century businessperson looking for an investment option, international trade was what was hot. Fortunes could be made importing spices, sugar, molasses, and tobacco into Europe from the Americas. Fortunes could also just as easily be lost in the long voyage across the Atlantic Ocean. These were risky investments. Pirates could swoop in and steal it all. A storm could send a ship full of valuable cargo to the bottom of the sea. Shipwreck at sea often meant debtors' prison for the businesspeople back home. An investor who had put all his money into a single shipload of goods could easily find himself and his family impoverished. Wise eighteenth-century businesspeople learned to divide their investments between several ships. That way, if one ship were lost at sea, the investors' financial security wouldn't be utterly destroyed.

Today's retirement funds are in a similar situation as those eighteenth-century ships. They're not facing pirates and storms at sea, of course. Instead, an aging workforce, a shaky economy, and Wall Street have endangered many workers' pensions. At this point, many of these funds are like leaky ships, sinking lower and lower into the waves. The folks whose retirement plans are carried by a single vessel—their employer's pension plan—may find themselves shipwrecked.

AGING WORKERS

More and more people have found that the pension plan they were counting on for their retirement isn't going to be quite what they thought it would be. This is what's happened to thousands of UPS employees. UPS is a successful company that earned more than $8 billion in 2014, but many of its employees' retirement packages were funded through a separate company, the Central States Pension Fund. In 2015, nearly nine thousand UPS retirees were told that their pensions would be cut in half.[20]

Central States Pension Fund covers hundreds of thousands of employees from other companies as well as UPS. As more and more workers retire, fewer and fewer working employees are left to contribute to the fund. In fact, Central States now has five retirees for every worker. To make matters worse, some of its contributing companies

---

20 David Moberg, "Central States Pension Fund Prepares to Spash Hundreds of Thousands of Workers' Pensions," October 5, 2015, http://inthesetimes.com/working/entry/18472/central_states_pension_fund_prepares_to_slash_hundreds_of_thousands_of_work.

have gone bankrupt. With shrinking funds, Central States sent letters to more than four hundred thousand members, warning that their benefits would be cut. Not everyone in the fund would have the same pension cuts. People who were over the age of eighty, on disability, or receiving a spousal death benefit would not see their checks cut at all, but others most definitely would. Those retirees whose employers left the fund without paying what was due on their employees' behalf would face the most severe cuts.

Sadly, Central States isn't the only pension fund that's found itself in this situation. Before a December 2014 federal law was passed, it was illegal for pension funds to cut benefits, but now the law allows for it when it's necessary to prevent the funding company's insolvency. It's a course of action that more and more pension funds are likely to take.

FAILING COMPANIES

The increasing numbers of retired people isn't the only thing that's nibbling away on pension funds. In today's shaky economy, several large businesses have been forced to go bankrupt. When they do, it doesn't only cost their current employees their jobs; it also endangers the pension funds to which the companies contributed.

In 2012, for example, when Hostess went bankrupt, it was bad news for its employees and retirees—and for Ottenberg's Bakery, which shared a pension plan with Hostess. With Hostess insolvent, unable to pay its retirees, Ottenberg's would have to pick up the tab. Ottenberg's older employees were afraid they would have to postpone retirement indefinitely.

In this case, the US government stepped in and saved Ottenberg's employees' pensions—at the cost of Hostess's employees, who got a reduced government-financed payout. But this situation isn't unique. The retirement security of more than ten million Americans depends on multiemployer pension plans. Having a large investment pool for pension funds was once believed to be a way to reduce risks, since financing didn't rely on a single company. Two recessions and industry consolidation prompted by deregulations have proved the fallacy of this belief. Dozens of multicompany pension funds have already failed, changing the lives of their ninety-four thousand participants.

THE STOCK MARKET

The aging workforce and failing contributing companies are significant factors that put employer pension funds at risk, but the stock market also plays a role. As the market recovers from its lows, many retirement plans will do the same—but some won't!

Unlike their counterparts in the private sector, state and local public pension funds have been allowed to assume they will hit nearly unachievable investment return targets based upon strategies that involve high risk, high fees, and general underperformance, while discounting their liabilities accordingly. Meanwhile, promises are being made to pensioners that can't be delivered, because of underperforming assets and high fees.

In Pennsylvania in 2015, the unfunded liability exceeded $50 billion. The $53 billion Pennsylvania State Teachers fund, which covers more than six hundred thousand workers and retirees, has 62 cents for every $1 in promised benefits. The $27 billion State Employees Retirement System fund, which covers more than

230,000 workers and retirees, has an $18 billion deficit. It has about 59 cents for every $1 in benefits it is obligated to pay.[21]

Pennsylvania isn't alone. In fact, in January 2016, *Forbes* magazine reported that some states—such as Illinois with $195 billion in unfunded liabilities, California with $180 billion, Texas with $123 billion, and New Jersey with $85 billion—exceed Pennsylvania's deficit, while other states—such as Massachusetts with $61 billion and Connecticut with $53 billion in unfunded liabilities—fare slightly better than Pennsylvania.[22]

Corporations' pension funds are also in big trouble. The ten worst public companies with unfunded liabilities are Motorola, Connoco Phillips, and Exxon Mobil (all about 64 percent); Entergy (62 percent); Goodyear, Sears, and General Dynamics (all 60 percent); American Airlines (57 percent); United/Continental (47 percent); and United Airlines (38 percent). Verizon advertises that it has the best wireless network in the USA, and meanwhile, it has an unfunded pension liability of $8.5 billion.[23]

When pension plans become so underfunded, it's inevitable that benefits will have to be cut. We can't stick our heads in the sand any longer. The markets will not allow retirement plans to recoup the billions they need, and neither companies nor governments can afford to simply put the missing money into the plans.

---

21 "Public Pensions Watch 2015," Actuarial Outpost, http://www.actuarialoutpost.com/actuarial_discussion_forum/showthread.php?t=288895.

22 William Baldwin, "State Pension Funds: As Broke as Ever," *Forbes*, January 15, 2016, http://www.forbes.com/sites/baldwin/2016/01/16/state-pension-funds-as-broke-as-ever/#5a216ac54900.

23 "Worst funded corporate pension plans," *Pensions & Investments*, April 30, 2013, http://www.pionline.com/gallery/20130430/SLIDESHOW2/430009998/1.

PLAN B

What would you do if you were living on a $4,000-per-month pension and were notified that your monthly pension would now be $2,000? It would be a life-changing event, that's for sure. You might have to go back to work. Your spouse might have to put off retiring. But what if you and your spouse had health issues that prevented you from working? Your only option would be to make major lifestyle adjustments.

This is a situation that more and more retirees are being forced to face. So what can you do to keep it from happening to you? Well, if you're able to take a lump-sum payout on your employee pension plan, that could be a good idea. If you can't take a lump-sum payout, you'll need a backup plan in case your pension plan runs out of money.

Changes are coming, and thinking your pension will always be there is just waiting for trouble to arrive. Think like those eighteenth-century investors in the transatlantic trade: hope for the best, but plan for the worst.

And don't worry. We're going to tell you how to create your Plan B. But first, we're going to tell you where you *shouldn't* turn for retirement security.

FACT
A pension fund no longer guarantees
a secure retirement.

CHAPTER 4

FACT OR FICTION:

WALL STREET AND THE BROKERAGE
INDUSTRY HAVE ALL THE ANSWERS

The shell game has been around for a long, long time. You know how it works. Three or more identical containers (which may be cups, shells, bottle caps, or anything else) are placed upside down with some small object hidden inside one of them. The containers are quickly shuffled, and one or more players are invited to bet on which container hides the object. Everything is done in plain sight, so it seems that the players' chances of choosing correctly are fairly high.

Unfortunately, that's not the way the shell game works. When the game is played honestly, the operator can consistently win if he shuffles the containers in a way that the players can't follow. Where it's played dishonestly—which is often the case—a con man rigs the game using sleight-of-hand to always create a losing outcome for the player. Of course, smart scammers allow players to win just enough to convince them that they're playing a legitimate game. Once they're psychologically hooked, the con artist has them where he wants them.

Historians say the shell game dates back at least as far as ancient Greece. It became very popular during the nineteenth century, when games were often set up at traveling fairs. (The fact that the shell men never stayed in one place very long kept them out of jail.) Today the game is still being played for money in many major cities around the world, even though it's illegal in most countries.

The shell game is also being played today in another form, a far more sophisticated form. It's called the stock market.

WALL STREET'S FALSE INFORMATION

In the stock market's version of the shell game, players are led to believe they can win at the game. They may, in fact, win enough to get them hooked, but in the end, they invariably lose. That's partly because other "players" are actually in on the scam.

Wall Street has sophisticated propaganda machines, but so do some of the other players in the game. Large brokerage firms broadcast the impression that their industry is in competition with the stock market. That's not actually the case. Instead, the brokerage industry is blocking a consumer revolution that would bring much-needed vigor and freshness to our economy. It's working hand-in-hand with Wall Street, and it's the investors who pay the cost for the brokerage firms' enormous wins.

The stock market ought to be a serviceable piece of infrastructure, much like a public utility. Its function should be to aggregate capital and then distribute it where the economy needs it most, not put its money where it will benefit Wall Street the most, creating financial instruments that exist solely for its own benefit. These financial firms act as toll bridges between investors and entrepreneurs, and the tolls they levy mean that an enormous percentage of businesses' profits go straight to brokers' bonuses.

A CONFLICT OF INTERESTS

Selling mutual funds is complicated. If you go to a financial advisor and ask him to create a mutual-fund investment plan for you, he will have about eight thousand publicly available mutual funds in a variety of share classes to choose from. To find what he thinks is the right match for you, he'll use as many as twenty-two sources and characteristics, ranging from fund rankings and tax efficiency to fund risk and manager tenure. Since the process is so complicated, you may just feel grateful that there's someone to help you out who knows the ins and outs. You know your advisor's decisions are based on objective criteria, so you leave the whole thing in his hands because . . . well, because you may not really understand much about what he's doing. What you probably don't know is that the objective criteria your financial advisor bases his decisions on were compiled by a fund company that makes cash payments to those advisors who sell their funds to clients. It's called revenue sharing, and it's common practice.

The US Securities and Exchange Commission (SEC) defines revenue sharing as occurring when payments are exchanged between advisors and brokers or dealers. In some cases, these payments are called reimbursements for expenses incurred while selling the shares. Even so, these payments give the broker or advisor an incentive to sell the shares of funds that pay revenue sharings versus those that don't, regardless of which funds are actually best for their clients.

Because the entire mutual-fund scenario is so opaque and complex, many investors don't understand that revenue sharing and other fees are industry practice. Very few advisors explain the facts to investors, even though they have a fiduciary relationship with their clients. Meanwhile, unknown to the investors, revenue sharing and fees are taking a chunk out of their net returns.

Before you invest in mutual funds, keep these three points in mind:

- the complexity of most forms of compensation between your advisor, his broker, and a fund distribution company

- the lack of transparency that keeps you from being able to clearly see these compensation arrangements

- the difficulty your advisor faces even if she wants to explain complicated compensation arrangements to you in an understandable way

It's to the brokerage industry's advantage to keep things the way they are. But it wasn't always like this. Back in 1948, brokerage and financial industries accounted for roughly 8 percent of all domestic corporate profits. According to the Bureau of Economic Analysis, this percentage bounced up and down around 10 percent until 1985, and then it starting rising. By 2003, the brokerage industry was raking in 40 percent of all the profits of all the public companies in America. This figure dropped to under 10 percent during the economic crisis of 2008 and then quickly rose to 30 percent again by 2012.[24]

---

24 Bureau of Economic Analysis, "Measuring the Nation's Economy," https://www.bea.gov.

Why does our government allow this to happen? Well, Wall Street spends far, far more than consumer advocates do on congressional campaigns and lobbyists. And the government has its own part to play in the problem.

THE GOVERNMENT'S ROLE

Not all the money that rightfully belongs to investors goes into brokerage firms' pockets. It may look as though the government is placing well-deserved penalties on the large investment firms, but most of those settlements don't do private investors any good. Instead, the money goes straight into the US Treasury Department's hungry maw, where it's used to pay down the nation's debt and offset a whole bunch of unspecified government expenditures.

So what are those unspecified expenditures? Well, that's a very good question, and the answer is far from clear. In a Fox Business news article, Harvey Pitt, former Securities and Exchange Commission chairman, stated, "When this money is obtained, where it goes, what it's used for, how it's dealt with is something most members of the public would want to know and should be told." He added, "It ought to be possible for the Treasury to report on what it does with the money given the amounts in question."[25]

How much money are we talking about? A lot. In fact, between 2010 and 2013, US bank-holding companies paid more than $85 billion in settlements with federal regulators, according to figures compiled by SNL Financial. Some of that money did, in fact, go to the investors who were harmed by the financial institutions' actions, but most was swallowed up by the US Treasury Department.

25 Dunstan Prial, "Huge Wall Street Fines Raise Calls for More Transparency," Fox Business, June 13, 2013, http://www.foxbusiness.com/politics/2014/06/13/huge-wall-street-fines-raise-calls-for-more-transparency-1287760936.html.

In a Fox Business news article, James Cox, a professor of law at Duke University and an expert in corporate and securities regulation, stated that "the public knows as much about where that money goes as they do where their tax dollars go." Cox acknowledged that some of the money does benefit taxpayers, but how and how much is far from clear: "It's the old shell game. Money is fungible."[26]

In other words, the government can switch the "ball" from shell to shell, and the "players" (private investors) won't be able to see what's happening. In the past, the size of that "ball" might have been so small that no one really cared all that much where it ended up. "But today," to quote Securities and Exchange Commission Chairman Harvey Pitt, "with the numbers we're seeing, this is very serious money. Without people knowing what it's used for, a multitude of sins can be buried . . . To my way of thinking, this is something people ought to know about and have a right to know about."[27]

Investors think that real profits can be gained from the stock market's shell game, but here are the facts that are actually hidden inside the game. First, in the world of independent broker-dealers, reps wear "fiduciary hats" when they're giving advice to investors, and then they whip that hat off and replace it with a "sales hat." Unfortunately, investors aren't aware that their brokers have two hats or that their brokers' contradictory hats mean that investors' best interests are not being served.

Investors are confused. Wall Street firms' brokers and representatives call themselves various things—"financial advisors," "investment advisors," and "wealth managers"—that imply they're working for the investor. Sophisticated advertising enhances that impression.

---

26 Ibid
27 Ibid

A study released by the Rand Corporation and sponsored by the SEC found that most consumers don't know whether they are working with a broker or an advisor.[28] They don't even know the difference between the two or what they should expect from each.

This is only the tip of the iceberg when it comes to the problem of the brokerage industry's relationship with Wall Street. The deeper you go beneath the surface, the more details are revealed, proving that the stock market is one of the worst places to invest your hard-earned retirement funds.

Bob Veres, in his *Advisor Perspectives* blog, uses strong language when he talks about Wall Street's deceptive business practices. He says they are "undermining consumer protections, engaging in anti-competitive behavior against the emergent financial-advisory profession, exerting undue and improper influence on Congress and the regulators, raking in excess profits and thereby harming the American economy that it originally was created to benefit."[29] Veres concludes the situation is so bad that it merits the death penalty. He tells his readers to work for "a society and economy that doesn't include brokerage firms at all," and he insists that "there are other parties who can do the jobs that Wall Street currently performs better, more ethically, more efficiently, and more beneficially to our economy as a whole."

When you look at the stock market's iconic symbol, Wall Street's powerful and muscular bull, it doesn't seem possible that the whole structure is so flawed. But we can assure you that it is. The stock market's system deliberately works against consumers' best interests, while at the same time putting pressure on the government to allow

28 *Study on Investment Advisers and Broker-Dealers*, US Securities and Exchange Commission, January 2011.
29 Bob Veres, "The Case against Wall Street," *Advisor Perspectives*, December 22, 2015, http://www.advisorperspectives.com/articles/2015/12/22/the-case-against-wall-street.

it to continue to rack up profits that damage the very economy it's supposed to support.

MISLEADING INFORMATION

Mutual-fund advertisements make lots of claims. Here are just a few:

- We help investors pursue their goals.

- Our expert managers have proven success rates.

- Investing systematically in our mutual funds will help you reach your target.

- Our portfolio managers have helped countless investors find the right mix of investments. They can help you build a brighter tomorrow.

- Our track record is unmatched.

According to Dow Jones's MarketWatch, if mutual-fund companies were truly honest with their shareholders, their ads would tell a quite different story. They'd include these far more accurate statements:[30]

- Our fund is much riskier than you think.

- If we experience a bear market and most of the stocks in your portfolio sink in value, that's just too bad. We won't even try to protect your money, because that's not our job.

- Sure we have a great track record, but that was then, and this is now. The manager who created our record left for a better-paying job.

---

30 "7 Mutual Fund Ads You'll Never See," MarketWatch, June 19, 2013, http://www.marketwatch.com/story/7-mutual-fund-ads-youll-never-see-2013-06-19.

- Actually, our great track record was largely the result of owning one stock that had a phenomenal return. Now we have attracted so much new money, it's virtually impossible to duplicate our success.

- Our five-star Morningstar rating is nice, but it doesn't mean what you think. In fact, it doesn't mean much at all for you.

- While we were achieving a terrific track record, most of our shareholders lost money.

- Our fund family's overall track record isn't anywhere near as good as it looks, because we can—and do—manipulate funds in order to improve our statistics.

Mutual funds are required by law to warn investors that their past performance is no guarantee of future performance. They also have to say that diversification won't protect investors against market risk. But they don't put that information in their advertisements. (You're much more likely to find it in their small print.)

Before the dot-com bubble burst, many mutual-fund companies grabbed up new tech companies' funds and persuaded their investors to buy into them. The companies knew something their investors didn't, though: the bubble was about to burst. More than fifteen years later, the companies still aren't being honest with their investors. As the MarketWatch article concludes, many companies should put in their prospectus this statement about their investments, which would be far more accurate: "Our portfolio owns lots of technology stocks, and historically, this asset class has suffered losses up to 80 percent from time to time. You should not invest in this fund unless you are willing to lose more than half your money."

By law, mutual funds are required to own at least twenty stocks, and most funds own somewhere between fifty and three hundred. The theory is that with so many stocks, one or two failures won't ruin overall investments. If the market were to decline 20 percent or more (which is what happens during a bear market), the losses become much more noticeable. When 85 percent or more of a mutual fund's stocks lose money, investors find themselves facing serious market risk. Very few mutual-fund managers do anything to protect their investors against this risk. Shareholders think that their fund managers will be doing all they can to shore up their investments, but the truth is, they're not. Legally, they're not even required to try.

Mutual-fund companies also like to brag about their expert managers. But they don't like to tell shareholders when their skilled portfolio managers leave to find other jobs. To avoid investors losing faith if they should get wind of manager turnovers, many funds now have committees that manage their funds. This makes their track record much more anonymous.

When it comes to an actively managed mutual fund, bigger usually isn't better.

Initially, superior results will bring in an influx of new money. More money often leads to the fund owning more companies and holding larger companies. This in turn reduces their flexibility, and it inflates the cost when they need to move in or out of a market.

Investors are usually impressed by Morningstar's ratings, and mutual funds play them up in their marketing. You need to keep in mind, however, that these ratings tell you nothing about future performance; they only measure a fund's past performance. Multiple studies have shown that a high Morningstar rating has very little value when it comes to predicting a fund's future.

During the early part of the twenty-first century, international stock returns were much higher than America's. Mutual funds with up to a quarter of their portfolios in international stocks could boast about their great performance, all the while implying to their investors that they held mostly US stock. If you separated out their international holdings, however, you'd have found that their actual record was, at best, only average.

Researchers have been tracking the flow of dollars in and out of funds for many years. What they've discovered is that average shareholders' returns are a very different number from the funds' returns. This is because most investors are impressed when prices rise and discouraged when they go down. As a result, they're more likely to buy when there's an increase in prices and sell after prices decline, which is the opposite of "buy low, sell high." Mutual funds tell their investors to "stay the course," but they don't stop people from making foolish decisions to buy. After all, it's to the funds' advantage when shareholders' money pours in.

What's, maybe, worst of all when it comes to evaluating a mutual fund's performance is that the company's success doesn't necessarily equate with shareholder profits. Throughout the first decade of the twenty-first century, the mutual-fund company CGM Focus, which invests mostly in real estate, reported an annual return of 17.8 percent. When Morningstar tracked the cash in and cash out of this fund, it found that average investors were actually losing 16.8 percent annually.[31]

---

31 Morningstar, "CGM Focus Fund," http://performance.morningstar.com/fund/performance-return.action?t=CGMFX.

IN A NUTSHELL

In the next chapter, we'll look even more deeply into the murky investment industry. For now, we hope that when you hear the hype the brokerage industry broadcasts, you'll remember the truth: the brokerage industry runs a shell game you don't want to play. It's hidden the facts from you, but when you pick a "shell," hoping for a major win, odds are good that shell will turn out to be empty. Why risk your money in a game that's rigged?

FACT

The brokerage industry is ethically and functionally flawed.

CHAPTER 5

FACT OR FICTION:
YOU KNOW WHERE YOUR MONEY
GOES IN YOUR INVESTMENT FUND

I t's hard to imagine a world without money. If you're like most people, you think about money at least once every day, and odds are good you spend a significant portion of your waking hours thinking about your finances. Our concept of dollars and cents shapes our ideas about life and happiness, about relationships and family, and about security and the future. But if you had been alive eleven thousand years or so ago, your reality would have been very different from what it is today in the twenty-first century. Human nature would have been about the same, but instead of thinking about your bank account and investments, you would have been thinking about the cattle in your fields.

Cattle were one of the earliest forms of money. Their value could be standardized (for example, four goats might equal one cow). They could also be accumulated: the more cattle you had, the wealthier you were. Furthermore, their value remained, regardless of whether you had them on your person; wealth could be stored in fields. Last, and best of all, cattle were an investment. Because cows and goats naturally reproduce, a herd of cattle would become bigger—and more valuable—the longer you had it.

As a form of wealth investment, however, cattle had a few problems. Suppose you are the chieftain of your tribe. This means you're a wealthy man with many cattle, but it also means you're obliged to lead your men to war. While you're gone, your cattle remain in your fields, entrusted to the care of other members of your tribe. These are people you've known for years. You trust them absolutely, so when you return from war, after a couple of years, you expect to find many more cows grazing your fields, but instead, you discover that your herd is about the same size as it was when you left. What happened? You suspect the people who were caring for the cattle robbed you, but they deny it. They insist that those two years were just bad for cattle. Many of the calves died. It was nobody's fault really, they tell you, and they insist they did the best they could. In reality, though, the men you trusted have been building their own herds, stealing cows from your pastures. As the tribal chieftain, you might decide to put the scoundrels to death. But that won't get your cattle back!

In the modern world, you may find yourself in a similar situation with your investment fund. You've put your wealth there, expecting to find that it will increase significantly. When it doesn't, you're not sure whom to blame. You don't really understand what happened. No matter how angry you are, there's not much you can do. You thought you knew exactly where your money was going when you put it into your investment fund. But you didn't.

HOW FEES CAN AFFECT YOUR PORTFOLIO

Mr. Jones is a client of ours who found himself in this situation. He had invested $1 million in a variable annuity. When we first met with him, he said he was paying only 1 percent each year on this variable annuity. We shook our heads sadly and told him that his advisor hadn't been fully truthful with him.

"But I've know this guy for years," he said. "I trust him. How can you doubt his honesty when you don't even know him?"

We suggested he make a phone call, not to the broker but, rather, to the insurance company that had issued the variable annuity.

"All right," Mr. Jones said, his tone grudging. "But you'll see that I'm right and you're wrong."

The call was made on speakerphone, so we heard the customer-service rep ask the appropriate questions to verify Mr. Jones's identity. Once she was satisfied that Mr. Jones was who he said he was, she asked, "What can I help you with today, Mr. Jones?"

"I want to know what fees I'm paying on my annuity," he told her.

"Okay," she said. "Let me see . . . Here we are. You're paying insurance fees, including mortality expenses, of 1.65 percent, and investment or mutual fund fees of 1.9 percent. That includes your 1 percent fee to your broker. And then you are also paying rider fees of 1.5 percent."

Mr. Jones was paying 5.05 percent in fees each year! He had trusted his broker, and now, just like that long-ago tribal chieftain we had you pretend to be, he'd learned the truth, the hard way.

To make things worse, Mr. Jones isn't a wealthy man; he's a retired teacher who never made more than $40,000 a year before he retired. Now this variable annuity was making more in fees each year than Mr. Jones had ever earned in his working career. This meant he wasn't seeing his investment grow the way he'd hoped. Say the market were to go up 10 percent. In that case, he would only earn 4.95 percent because the company would take its 5.05 percent. If the market were to go down 10 percent, his loss would be even greater: he would lose a total of 15.05 percent (10 percent market loss plus 5.05 percent fees).

Don't make the mistake Mr. Jones did. Don't go away and leave your wealth in a broker's hands, trusting him to increase your investment on your behalf. Instead, keep a close eye on your investment expenses. Ask questions. Get a second opinion. Consider other options! Variable annuity expenses will not only shrink your investment; they'll also endanger your retirement plans. They'll put your lifetime goals at risk.

You may think a percent more here and there won't make that much difference. You'd be surprised how those percentages add up over time and what a big bite they can take out of your nest egg!

Let's say you have a $100,000 investment in a mutual fund that's earning 4 percent. Without any fees, your portfolio would have grown to almost $220,000 over the next twenty years. But let's say you have even the minimal 1 percent fee Mr. Jones thought he had on his variable annuity. That 1 percent would subtract almost $28,000 from your portfolio. Keep in mind that if that $28,000 hadn't been lost, it would have been reinvested at the same rate as the rest of your portfolio. This means an additional loss of $12,000. In other words, if you take into consideration both the direct cost of the fee and the money you could have earned if the fee had been reinvested, even a

1 percent fee adds up to almost $40,000 over twenty years. That's about a third of the total $120,000 return that should have been yours on your investment.

Of course, if you had twenty "good years," when your money earned more, you might not feel so upset about the money you lost to fees. But in fact, there are plenty of years when investment returns are actually less than 4 percent. During those times, you'll be hurting a lot more! That "tiny" 1 percent will have multiplied your loss.

The sad truth, as Mr. Jones discovered, is that most investment vehicles have fees that are a good deal higher than 1 percent. According to a recent figure from Morningstar, the average annual fee for mutual funds is 1.26 percent. This is called the expense ratio. If you have a mutual fund, you need to find out what your expense ratio is sooner rather than later, before too much of your hard-earned money has been bled away. By law, the expense ratio has to be listed in the mutual fund's prospectus as the total annual fund-operating expense. But your expense ratio still won't give you the full picture! There are many other types of fees and expenses.

The SEC breaks these down into two broad categories: transaction fees (what is paid to a brokerage firm when stock is first bought) and continuing fees or expenses (which includes, but isn't limited to, the expense ratio). Here are just a few transaction fees:

- *Markup:* This is just what it sounds like—when a brokerage firm sells you securities, it is holding at a price that's higher than the actual market price.

- *Sales loads:* Some mutual funds charge these in a variety of ways. Front-end loads are paid when you first make an investment, while back-end loads are charged when you sell it.

- *Surrender charges:* If you withdraw early from a variable annuity, you'll be charged a surrender charge.

The SEC also identified these continuing fees:

- *Investment advisory fees:* Advisors charge these as payment for their services. They're often based on the size of the portfolio; the larger it is, the more you'll pay.
- *401(k) fees:* These are additional expenses for operating and administering retirement plans, and they're often passed on to employees (that's on top of funds' other fees).

The SEC cautions that this list doesn't include every fee that you may be paying on your investment. You could, for example, be charged additional fees if you don't maintain a minimum balance. You might also be paying for account "maintenance," transfer, or inactivity. The fund may require that you shoulder legal costs, taxes, and monitoring or oversight fees, as well as other expenses charged to the portfolio companies held in a fund. It gets complicated!

FEE-ONLY VERSUS FEE-BASED

Some other terms that confuse investors are "fee-only" and "fee-based." A fee-only broker would receive *only* his fees and no commissions or sales-related revenues. A fee-based broker, however, is able to receive generous commissions, bonuses, and perks based on his sales. In other words, he can still switch back and forth between his two hats as both a private investor's advisor and as a broker who benefits from his sales.

Fee-based accounts have been with us for a long time. Since their introduction in the mid-1980s, fee-based accounts have received both criticism and praise. Some of these fees are appropriate. If you are a trader or generate numerous transactions in your account, a flat fee-based account may make a great deal of sense in lieu of your paying individual commissions per each trade. Another sensible example of having a fee-based account is in hiring a professional money manager since, often, the fee charged reflects the cost for hiring this person in the first place. The broker may also add his hiring fee to this type of account, which is also acceptable if the fees are not too excessive. Your broker or financial advisor may offer you a fee-based mutual-fund account, which makes sense if you need the help and direction to manage your account with an entire portfolio of mutual funds. In this situation, however, the fees may be high, and there can be some serious hidden dangers, including the fact that a fee-based account doesn't insure against loss in a market correction.

In our experience, we have met with people who are about to retire or are already in retirement, and we often find that they are invested in some type of fee-based account where the invested portfolios are risky, including unsuitable stocks and/or mutual funds. We have also met many individuals with significant portfolios who are paying fees in excess of 2 percent annually. They are completely at risk if the market underperforms or crashes. The justification given is that their portfolios are diversified, and allocations are made frequently. However, the reality is that when someone retires, a more conservative approach should be taken, and fees and risk should be constantly addressed and consistently justified.

We are seeing more and more abuses with fee-based accounts. Accounts that are supposed to be fixed-income accounts are not. Individuals who need an income to live on and who cannot afford to take any risks are unknowingly totally invested in mutual funds, requiring them to pay high fees.

What's even worse is that while many clients rely on that income to live on, their portfolios contain fixed-income mutual funds, also known as bond funds, which pay them less income each year than they are paying in annual fees. When interest rates begin to go up, the funds' values could decline. For example, a $500,000 portfolio may be charged $12,500 annually, while the account has generated only $6,000 in total income, less than half of what the investor is paying in fees.

Another common scenario is someone with a bond portfolio who is charged a fee between 2 percent and 2.5 percent, a rate that is higher than the interest rate on a majority of the bonds in this person's portfolio. While this action is not illegal, it *is* unethical. A bond is meant to be an income-producing vehicle used to pay a certain interest return for a designated period of time. At bond maturity, the investor expects to receive money. However, when the portfolio is static—meaning the advisor hasn't done any additional work after researching and purchasing the bonds—there's no reason to charge an annual fee any longer. Why would you pay your advisor an annual fee when all he's doing is mailing you the interest checks once they're received?

Finally, the worst possible situation we see is when an investor is charged a fee for all the assets in an account, even if a large portion of the money is in a money-market account. Once again, this is not illegal, but it is exceedingly unethical.

Bottom line? While fee-based accounts can make sense in some specific instances, you should always be aware of the abuses that often occur with them. After all, it's your hard-earned money.

IT'S HARD TO KNOW WHAT
YOU DON'T KNOW

If you find all of this confusing, you're not alone. The brokerage firms aren't eager to help anyone understand more easily. Many of their charges are intentionally hidden from view. A 2015 report from CEM Benchmarking, a Toronto-based consulting fund that specializes in analyzing the performance of pension funds, estimated that more than half of all the costs charged to US pension funds aren't disclosed to investors.[32] Those undisclosed charges cost you. The difference between what funds reported as expenses and what they actually charged, CEM reported, averaged at least 2 percentage points a year. The bigger your portfolio, the greater the loss; if you had a $3 billion portfolio, the loss would add up to $61 million. CEM pointed out that their estimates are conservative; odds are good that most investors are paying more than that. A 2009 research study, for example, found that the average private-equity fund charged more than 7 percent a year in fees.[33]

How do investment firms get away with this? Well, for one thing, they take advantage of loopholes in their accounting laws. They're supposed to report "investment-related costs" if they can be separated from "investment income and the administrative cost of the pension plan." The firms get to decide which fees are "separable," which allows them to conceal many of the fees they're charging investors.

Vanguard's John Bogle wants investors to stop brokers and financial advisors from profiting at their expense. In a 2015 *Time*

32 *The Time Has Come for Standardized Total Cost Disclosure for Private Equity*, CEM Benchmarking, April 2015, http://www.cembenchmarking.com/Files/Documents/CEM_article_-_The_time_has_come_for_standardized_total_cost_disclosure_for_private_equity.pdf.
33 Ludovic Phalippou, "Beware of Venturing into Private Equity," *The Journal of Economic Perspectives*, Vol. 23, No. 1 (Winter, 2009), 147–166.

interview, he reported that $32 trillion in securities changes hands every year with no real profit for investors. "The job of finance is to provide capital to companies. We do it to the tune of $250 billion a year in IPOs [initial public offerings] and secondary offerings," Bogle said. "What else do we do?" he continued, "We encourage investors to trade about $32 trillion a year. So the way I calculate it, 99 percent of what we do in this industry is people trading with one another, with a gain only to the middleman. It's a waste of resources."[34]

TOLL TAKERS AND CAR SALESPEOPLE

MarketWatch's Mitch Tuchman points out that this $32 trillion is nearly double the entire US economy.[35] That means that the stock market is moving that enormous sum from one pocket to another, with what Tuchman calls a "toll-taker" in the middle, someone who just collects money without having to do any actual work.

A toll road that is never traveled doesn't collect money. You need lots of travelers if you want to generate lots of income. So if you think of stockbrokers as toll takers, you can see what their incentives are: to get as many investors as possible to be actively trading in the stock market. An account that sits invested for months with no trades is a dead weight. Brokers need *action*—and it matters nothing to their earnings whether that action accomplishes anything positive for investors.

"Research shows, over and over," Tuchman said in an August 2015 article, "that stock brokers can't do much of anything demonstrably valuable. They don't know which stocks will go up or down

---

34 Pat Regnier, "Jack Bogle Explains How the Index Fund Won with Investors," *Money*, July 27, 2015, http://time.com/money/3956351/jack-bogle-index-fund.
35 Mitch Tuchman, "Why 99% of Trading Is Pointless," MarketWatch, August 1, 2015, http://www.marketwatch.com/story/why-99-of-trading-is-pointless-john-bogle-2015-07-30.

and when. They don't know which asset classes will outperform this year or next. Nobody knows."[36]

He continued:

> If you're among that small cadre of extremely high-level traders who can throw loads of cash at a short-term fluke, fantastic. If you have a mind for numbers like Warren Buffett that allows you to buy companies on the cheap and hold them forever, excellent. If you're a normal retirement investor trying to get from A to B and retire on time, well, you have a really big problem to face: the toll-taker wants your money.

Stockbrokers make money by getting investors to make trades. Despite what you might think, they don't actually get paid for their advice. Their goal isn't to make their clients' investments grow as much as possible. Instead, they make money by persuading investors to keep their accounts active and constantly moving. That way brokers and advisors can rack up commissions for themselves and their employers. Maybe a better metaphor for brokers would be sleazy car salespeople who just want to move the inventory, regardless of whether the cars are safe and reliable!

When you buy a car, though, at least you can do some negotiating with the salesperson. You can try to get the best deal you can. But imagine that when you bought a car, the dealership refused to tell you what you were paying for. What if the salesperson said, "I can't really tell you what will and won't be on your car when you drive it home." When you settled on a price, you'd have no idea whether it was a good deal or a bad deal. Of course, you'd never stand for this

---

36 Ibid.

when it comes to buying a car. You'd take your business to another dealer. But when it comes to your investments in variable annuities and mutual funds, you accept this situation.

The job of a financial advisor is to provide advice. Do you actually get that from your broker? And if you do, is it worth anything?

WHY PAY TO LOSE?

Your broker may try to convince you that his services are well worth the extra fees. "I can get you a higher return," he might promise, "so the extra fees will pay off to your advantage." Chances are that's not true. Bogle likes to say that, when it comes to investing, "You get what you don't pay for."

To put this into perspective, a portfolio that's yielding 2.5 percent while being charged a 1 percent fee has an overall net return of 1.5 percent. In other words, you're paying someone for doing you the service of taking your money. Why would you want to do that? Believe us, that tribal chieftain would never have rewarded the cattle thieves by willingly giving them a few more cows!

FACT

Many private-equity firms have hidden costs that are robbing your investment.

CHAPTER 6

FACT OR FICTION:
AVERAGE STOCK-MARKET RETURNS TELL AN ACCURATE STORY

Nineteenth-century drug companies didn't face the stiff regulations they do today. Instead, when they sold their products, they were allowed to tell consumers pretty much whatever they wanted. Snake-oil salesmen made outrageous claims about their products, promising cures for everything from alcoholism to stiff muscles, from upset stomachs to "melancholy."

In 1885, for example, one company promoted the Health Jolting Chair in an advertisement that skillfully presented a persuasive mixture of truths, exaggerations, and outright lies.[37]

---

37 US National Library of Medicine, ihm.nlm.nih.gov/luna/servlet/detail/
NLMNLM~1~1~101435627~139833:-Medical-instruments-and-apparatus-.

The chair was claimed:

- "to be suitable for all ages and most physical conditions." (Seems like a pretty unobjectionable claim.)

- "to be constructed in the very best manner . . . simple and durable." (Probably true.)

- "to be convenient, comfortable, and inexpensive." (Again, probably true.)

- "to be indispensable to the health and happiness of millions of human beings." (Well, that's pretty clearly an exaggeration!)

- "to cure corpulency if used in conjunction with a well-regulated diet." (Weight loss seems likely with pretty much any "well-regulated diet," so this squeaks by as an exaggeration.)

- "to be a household blessing." (It's hard to argue about what is and isn't a blessing.)

- "to cure constipation, dyspepsis . . . torpid liver and kidneys, nervousness . . . loss of appetite, sleeplessness, rheumatism, gout, neuralgia." (Now we've crossed the line into outright lies!)

- "to be a brain refresher for those engaged in . . . mental work, and a great remedy for the tired voice of voice-users." (A *chair* refreshes your brain and cures a hoarse voice? Really?)

When we read advertisements like this, we laugh. We can't imagine how our ancestors could have been so gullible that they believed such obvious exaggerations and lies. In a world where poor health had far fewer scientifically based cures, people believed what they *wanted* to believe.

We're no different today. Thanks to the FDA, we're no longer exposed to pharmaceutical advertising that contains blatant lies, but we don't have the same protection when it comes to the claims made by Wall Street and the brokerage industry. We want to believe in a world of possibility for getting rich.

WALL STREET'S SNAKE OIL

Investors seldom realize the lies they've been told. All the stock-market analyses they read make it look as if there's easy money to be made on Wall Street. Anyone can get rich. Or at least that's the story.

Too many investors get the wrong information from the wrong places. When the stock market soars to all-time highs (which it does from time to time), investors shouldn't be fooled. Instead, they should pay attention to the larger picture: the market's overall deterioration from the inside out. For example, if the market climbs higher but has lower volume, that means fewer and fewer stocks are actually participating. It may look as if you're seeing new highs, but that's an illusion.

There are many more indicators out there that tell us the stock market is in serious trouble, and yet investors are still being lured by the snake oil. "You can find prosperity and wealth!" shout the analysts and the brokers, and gullible investors put their money down. When the promises don't materialize, most investors (including many pros) will find themselves no better off than they were before—and quite possibly, worse.

EXAGGERATIONS AND MISDIRECTION

When the market looks bullish, it's hard to believe that another crash may be just around the corner. The snake-oil salesman sounds so credible. As investors watch earnings per share (EPS) climb, they feel as though the pattern will never end—until it does.

Investors need to ask themselves where the apparent growth is coming from. It's not from sales growth, because sales per share aren't growing much. That's because the economy itself isn't growing much, and economists predict that it won't for a while. And keep in mind that what growth we are seeing in gross domestic product (GDP) is driven by the creation of new enterprises, which indicates nothing about the sales of publically traded businesses that already exist.

So where is all that apparent market growth coming from? Mark Hulbert at MarketWatch saw two possible sources:

> One would be for the number of shares to fall dramatically, because of share repurchases and the like. Other things being equal, of course, fewer shares result in higher per-share numbers . . . Another way for EPS to grow faster than sales would be for profit margins to expand.[38]

Hulbert goes on to explain that both these arguments are fundamentally flawed. First, investors should be looking at net buybacks minus new shares issued; historically, corporations create new shares at a faster pace than they've repurchased them. And second, historically, when profit margins are at a record high, they revert to their long-term mean. This means that the arguments used to support a

---

38 Mark Hulbert, "Simple Math Does Not Support the Bulls," MarketWatch, October 23, 2013, www.marketwatch.com/story/simple-math-does-not-support-the-bulls-2013-10-23.

bullish market actually indicate that a change is in the air, one that will make a lot of people very unhappy.

When Hulbert added up the numbers, he warned, "You better be sitting down. The conclusion isn't pretty." His math indicated the following projections through 2018:

- *Sales per share will grow by only 2 percent annually.* And that's being optimistic, Hulbert warned. It assumes no share dilution caused by companies issuing more shares that they repurchase and that the GDP will have to grow faster than 2 percent annually in order for sales to live up to this.

- *Profit margins will revert only halfway from their current levels toward their long-term historical mean.* This also is a generous forecast, Hulbert warned again, because other experts have predicted that profit margins will fall even further than that.

- *The S&P 500's profit-earnings ratio will stay constant.* This again, Hulbert points out, may be too optimistic since the profit-earnings ratio is already above average, and things tend to revert to their average numbers rather than climb still higher.

Given these three predictions, which may err on the overly optimistic side, Hulbert concluded that, using simple math to calculate the numbers, the S&P 500 will be at 1,589 by 2018. Despite possible temporary ups and downs between now and then, that translates into an overall average loss between now and 2018.

Historically, the stock market has had an average growth of 10 percent per year. If we were to extend that out five years into the future, we'd be looking at a profit-earnings ratio that's over thirty. That's a number that hasn't happened very often, except during recessions, when earnings are lower than usual. In fact, Hulbert pointed out in his MarketWatch article that the only nonrecession occasion when that number has been reached since 1871 was in the months that lead to the dot-com bubble-burst in early 2000.

What does that tell us? That we could be in another bubble that will inevitably pop. Of course, no one knows the future. But do you really want to gamble your hard-earned retirement savings on something so risky? To make matters worse, the bullish markets' snake-oil projections aren't mere exaggerations; they may also be outright lies or at least intentional misdirection.

Another factor that has misled investors is that, despite all the claims that business is booming for US companies, they are actually deeply in debt. According to the Federal Reserve in 2015, nonfinancial corporate businesses owe 37 percent of the value of their net worth. If their stock prices drop, the value of the debt will still be there, as big as ever.

A 2015 analysis by investment bank SG Securities calculated that corporate America has "overspent" in recent years to the tune of hundreds of billions of dollars.[39] The analysis included these points:

- Since 2009, equity prices have almost doubled—but so has the net debt of nonfinancial companies. The cash pile of nonfinancial US corporations has risen by $570 billion, but debt has risen by $1.6 trillion.

39 Brett Arends, "Why Are Stock Prices So High? Follow the Borrowed Money," MarketWatch, May 7, 2015, www.marketwatch.com/story/why-are-stock-prices-so-high-follow-the-borrowed-money-2015-05-07.

- Net debt rose about 20 percent in the twelve-month period between August 2014 and August 2015, while gross cash flows rose only 4 percent.

- Those companies with the weakest sales growth are the ones that are buying back the most.

The net debt for most of the stock market is even worse than can be easily seen because the overall figure is skewed by a handful of companies (for example, Apple) with big cash piles. When you subtract those from the average, the overall picture looks even worse for the rest of the market.

Some people try to comfort themselves by pointing out that when you look at net debt levels compared with asset prices, things don't look so bad after all. But what if those prices are inflated? When companies report record profits, they may be touting misleading versions of their results, ignoring a whole range of normal business costs. Their adjusted profits leave out such things as costs related to laying off workers, a decline in the value of patents or other intangible assets, the value of company stock distributed to employees, or losses from a failed venture. Another number often missing in adjusted profit figures is the value of stock awarded to employees. Companies argue that because this stock-based pay requires no exchange of cash, it doesn't affect a company's earnings.

All of these are routine expenses that many businesses face, so it doesn't actually make much sense to overlook them. By doing so, however, companies make their profit margins look better than they actually are. And what's even worse, financial analysts are playing along with the sham. Instead of acting as truth finders, pushing the companies to report the actual numbers, analysts are pushing the same false advertising that the companies are.

The problem looks as if it's getting worse too. When the Associated Press (AP) analyzed the results from five hundred major companies, using 2015 data provided by a research firm S&P Capital IQ, it found that the gap between the adjusted profits companies were reporting and their bottom-line net income has been getting wider over the past five years. How wide has the gap become? Grand Canyon size! At more than one out of every five companies that the AP looked at (in other words, more than one hundred out of the five hundred), the adjusted profits were higher than their actual net income by 50 percent or more. Five years ago, many of these hundred companies weren't on the list, but they are now. Seventy-two percent of the companies had adjusted profits that were higher than net income in the first quarter of 2015, and adjusted earnings were, typically, 16 percent higher than net income. Fifteen of the hundred companies were actually losing money, even though their adjusted numbers implied that they were thriving.[40]

After the 2000 dot-com crash, companies and analysts promised to stop the exaggerations and lies. Regulations were put in place to make sure they kept their promises. Companies had to release detailed data for how they reached all their numbers. Instead of making profits more transparent, however, all the data became one more smokescreen. The numbers were confusing, and companies included so much unneeded data that it became nearly impossible to sift through it. Lynn Turner, the chief accountant at the SEC, commented in an AP news article that companies still put out "made-up, phony numbers" just as much as they did back in 2000—and maybe even more. "The analysts aren't doing enough to get behind the numbers

---

40 Bernard Condon, "AP Analysis: More 'Phony Numbers' in Reports as Stocks Rise," Associated Press, June 8, 2015, news.yahoo.com/experts-worry-phony-numbers-misleading-investors-070228914.html.

that management gives them to find out what's really going on," Turner pointed out.[41]

How do companies get away with this? Because it's perfectly legal—and sometimes even helpful—to present various ways at looking at profits. The goal, however, should not be to mislead investors but to help them gain insight into how a business is actually doing. Instead, investors are getting a smoke-and-mirrors version of the real state of affairs. They're pouring money into stocks that are not nearly as robust as they appear to be.

When you add up the differences between adjusted figures and net income, quarter after quarter and year after year, the discrepancies swell to dangerous proportions. Between 2010 and 2014, the AP found that the total adjusted profits for the S&P 500 were $583 billion higher than the sum of the actual bottom-line numbers.

Meanwhile, stocks are getting more expensive. The AP reported that in 2012 investors were paying $13.50 for every dollar of adjusted profits for companies in the S&P 500 index. That sounds bad enough, but in 2015, the number soared to nearly $18 paid by investors for every dollar of reported adjusted profits. This makes for a very shaky foundation for the stock market's apparent bullishness.

Here are some examples:

- Alcoa, the lightweight metals manufacturer, reported net losses of more than $900 million due to the cost of restructuring itself. However, analysts focus on the $3.1 billion in adjusted profits.

- Boston Scientific, a company that makes medical devices, had adjusted profits of $3.6 billion from 2010 through 2014. Looks good on paper. But when you subtract a

---

41 Ibid.

write-off for a failed acquisition, various restructuring costs, layoff costs, and the cost of lawsuits, you come up with a very different number. In fact, when you include those numbers in the picture, Boston Scientific had $4.9 billion in net losses.

- When Salesforce.com, a cloud-computing company, reports its profits to its investors, it routinely leaves out the cost of stocks given as a form of employee compensation. From 2010 to 2014, it reported $1.2 billion in adjusted profits. If you were to subtract stock pay and other costs, however, you'd be seeing a $712 million loss. [42]

These companies claim that the adjusted numbers actually give investors a better picture of the companies' financial health.

THE LIES INVESTORS TELL THEMSELVES

Michelle Leder, founder of Footnoted.com, which analyzes financial statements, told the AP that most investors don't bother to sift through the numbers. They don't put them together to get a full and clear image of the companies' stock value. Instead, they seize upon a single number—and it's often the wrong one. They're not much better than nineteenth-century Americans who eagerly bought the Health Jolting Chair because they were desperate for relief from their gout. Like them, today's investors believe what they want to believe.

After years of rising stock prices, investors see only that they're richer than they were before. They congratulate themselves for their wise investments. They gain confidence in the numbers companies report. And they really don't *want* to hear that those numbers don't

42 Ibid.

give a true picture. The fact is: investors lie to themselves as much as the companies do.

Jonathan Clements at MarketWatch listed these seven lies that investors tell themselves:[43]

1. *"I've beaten the market."* When investors look at their global stock portfolios, they'll likely see better performance than what the S&P 500 shows. If they can't find the favorable comparison they're hoping for, they may ignore one-year results and look only at three- or five-year returns. "Or," Clements states, "they might not use an index at all—and instead compare their results to the mediocre actively managed mutual funds their brother-in-law bought."

2. *"My stock picks have made so much money."* When investors see that their shares' prices have, on average, tripled since 2009, they give credit to their own market savvy. Based on that false confidence, they often trade too much and take large, undiversified gambles. As stocks appear to climb higher (based in large part on false numbers, of course), investors become even cockier. Any casino knows how this works: when gamblers feel as though they're playing with win money, they're more willing to risk it on the next bet. That's why casinos like to make sure gamblers "get lucky" at the start of the evening.

3. *"It's the Fed's fault."* If hefty returns don't materialize, investors don't like to blame their own foolishness. They'd rather put the blame elsewhere. As John Nofsinger, who wrote *The Psychology of Investing*, stated in Clements's MarketWatch article: "When our bond portfolios have

43 Jonathan Clements, "7 Lies Investors Tell Themselves," MarketWatch, May 26, 2015, www.marketwatch.com/story/7-lies-investors-tell-themselves-2015-05-25.

done well in recent years, it's because we made good decisions. But when it comes to the bond market's recent bad performance, we blame the fed." Or, as Nofsinger added, we may just rewrite the whole story in our favor: "We misremember to make ourselves feel better. We just ignore the fact that our 401(k) didn't do that well last year."[44]

4.   *"My portfolio has grown so much."* Investors may be looking at how much they've added to their portfolios from their savings rather than actual market growth. So long as they can find a positive number to focus on, though, they'll pick that one.

5.   *"It's only a paper loss."* Investors use their own faulty mental arithmetic to tally wins and losses. A loss is a loss, but by categorizing it as merely existing "on paper," investors manage to preserve their market-savvy self-image.

6.   *"I bought it for diversification."* This is another mental category investors use to hide losses from their own awareness. If an investment doesn't perform the way they hoped, they reclassify it as something that "might do well in another financial crisis."

7.   *"This time, I'll get out before the crash."* Hindsight is twenty-twenty. When we look back, the signs that the market was going to bottom out seem so obvious. Back then, before the last crisis and the one before that, investors were telling themselves the same lies they are telling today.

---

44 Jonathan Clements, "7 Lies Investors Tell Themselves," MarketWatch.

A rosy worldview is so much more pleasant than a bleak one. But sooner or later, reality will catch up with investors. Brian Rauscher, a chief portfolio strategist at Robert W. Baird & Co., told the AP that the stock market has a "bomb" hidden under it. "We don't know if the fuse is a few inches or a few miles," he said. But sooner or later, it *will* go off. It's inevitable.

BEFORE YOU INVEST IN THE STOCK MARKET

In April 2015 MarketWatch columnist Paul B. Farrell offered some warnings anyone should consider before deciding to invest in the stock market:[45]

- *As the market fluctuates more and more (in other words, its volatility increases), expect a high-risk rollercoaster ride.* In 2015, the financial company Bloomberg reported that the index created by Standard and Poor (known as the S&P) had gone up and down by 1 percent during a single day for fifteen sessions in a row. "Expect the wild ride to continue," Farrell warned.

- *Some investors who ignore warnings do win big, but don't bet that **you** will!* Remember that no matter how many times you win at a shell game, in the end, you'll always lose.

- *Market statistics can fuel investors' optimism, but these same statistics also mislead.* Statistics can be manipulated. You need to know the entire picture before you can interpret what the numbers truly indicate.

---

45 Paul B. Farrell, "It's a Game of Musical Chairs at the Wall Street Casino—And the Loser Is You," MarketWatch, April 3, 2015, www.marketwatch.com/story/its-a-game-of-musical-chairs-at-the-wall-street-casino-and-the-loser-is-you-2015-04-03.

- *Wall Street insiders are bad at picking winners, but they don't know they are.* In his book *Thinking Fast and Slow,* Daniel Kahneman, Nobel Prize-winning economist and psychologist and one of the developers of behavioral economics, stated that when it comes to picking stocks, Wall Street money managers' practices are "more like rolling dice than like playing poker." Their picks are "no more accurate than blind guesses." What's even worse, Kahneman noted, is that "this is true for nearly all stock pickers . . . whether they know it or not . . . and most do not."[46] You don't want a manager who doesn't know what he doesn't know!

- *Wall Street advice actually reduces your profits.* At an IA Compliance Summit, John C. Bogle, the founder of Vanguard, stated in his speech:

  > Our financial system is a greedy system, depending on high-transaction volumes, high leverage, and rank speculation to maximize its own rewards. As a result, it consumes far too large a share of the returns created by our business and economic system.

- *Day trading is a high-risk loser's game for a large percentage of all gamblers.* Again, at that summit, Bogle delivered the same message:

---

46 Daniel Kahneman, *Thinking Fast and Slow,* (New York: Farrar, Straus Giroux, 2011).

The financial system—the traders, the brokers, the investment bankers, the money managers, the middlemen, "Wall Street," as it were—takes a cut of all this frenzied activity, leaving investors as a group inevitably playing a loser's game. As bets are exchanged back and forth, our attempts to beat the market, and the attempts of our institutional money managers to do so, then, enrich only the croupiers, a clear analogy to our racetracks, our gambling casinos, and our state lotteries.[47]

Research backs up both Farrell's and Bogle's conclusions. A *Forbes* study reported that "North American Securities Administrators found that 77 percent of day traders lose money";[48] MarketWatch reported that 82 percent of all day traders lose money;[49] and a study by University of California finance professors Terry Odean and Brad Barber (who followed 66,400 Wall Street accounts for seven years) concluded, "The more you trade the less you earn," because of taxes and transaction costs.[50]

- Farrell concludes, in so many words, that trading is bad for your health, nerves, and family, in addition to your retirement plans!

47 John Bogle, "Building a Fiduciary Society," Bogle Financial Markets Research Center, March 13, 2009, www.vanguard.com/bogle_site/sp20090313.html.
48 "Day Trading El Dorado," Forbes, June 12, 2000.
49 Paul B. Farrell, "'Bull's-Eye Investors' Still Lose," MarketWatch, August 17, 2004, www.marketwatch.com/story/hitting-the-bulls-eye-and-losing-all-the-same.
50 Paul B. Farrell, "The More You Trade the Less You Earn," MarketWatch, August 6, 2001, http://www.marketwatch.com/story/the-more-you-trade-the-less-you-earn.

Don't fall for the stock market's snake oil. All the bullish data that's out there may have as shaky a foundation as the Health Jolting Chair's advertisement. It's based on a mixture of truths, exaggerations, and lies. You can do better than that when it comes to planning for your retirement!

FACT

Your actual stock-market returns will probably be far less than you expect.

CHAPTER 7

FACT OR FICTION:
THE ONLY WAY TO MAKE
MONEY IS TO RISK MONEY

Every year, billions of dollars pass through the casinos in Las Vegas. The promise of "winning big" lures people from all over the world. Unfortunately, most of those billions of dollars don't go back into the visitors' pockets. Instead, according to a 2013 study sponsored by the University of Las Vegas, Las Vegas's twenty-three casinos collectively brought in $5 billion of their visitors' money. On average, that's over $630,000 a day, per casino.[51] But that doesn't stop people from flocking to Las Vegas and laying their money down on the tables.

---

51 Libby Kane, "9 Tricks Casinos Use to Make You Spend More Money," *Business Insider*, August 19, 2014, http://www.businessinsider.com/how-casinos-make-you-spend-money-2014-8.

Las Vegas casinos use a variety of techniques for encouraging people to gamble. For one thing, they evade the truth about losses by advertising their payback rate: how much money people *aren't* losing in Las Vegas casinos. When a casino posts on a billboard "97.8 percent payback rate, highest in Reno!" they're not lying—technically. By law, Las Vegas casinos can't make claims that are outright false, but they take advantage of their visitors' gullibility and their willingness to forget something important: the "average payback rate" includes when someone wins megabucks in the casino, when there are slot tournaments, when someone wins a car. If you do the math, you'll see that the numbers seem to indicate that for every dollar the casino takes, it gives back 2.2 cents. If that's the case, when someone hits a million-dollar jackpot, how many dollars did it take to make that happen? The answer is just short of $45.5 million. No one does the math, though. Casinos are counting on that.

Casinos also give gamblers the illusion of control. If you visit Las Vegas, you get to choose which casino to visit, which games to play, and which moves to make. The more choices you have to choose from, the more you'll feel you're using your skills and intelligence to create your hoped-for outcome. Las Vegas gamblers get cocky. Casinos are counting on that too! When losses inevitably happen, gamblers tell themselves that bad luck is a fluke, one that they'll be able to overcome with more gambling. The more they risk, the more they're convinced they'll win.

Not many folks would say, "My retirement plan is to make it big in Las Vegas." Few people would be foolish enough to put their retirement savings in a slot machine or on a blackjack table. They don't realize that they're actually gambling when they put their money into mutual funds and other stock-market investments. And like all gamblers, they're convinced that the greater the risk is, the bigger their payback will be.

AMERICA'S LOVE AFFAIR
WITH FINANCIAL RISK

The last several decades have seen the rise of the individual investor, and most of these investors are convinced that investment equals some degree of risk. You can't expect your money to earn more money, they believe, without risking it. That's the nature of investment, they think. Now, as Americans have become more responsible for their own retirement, they've poured their money into various investment vehicles with as much faith as any Las Vegas gambler.

Half of the country's households now own shares directly or through mutual funds. Despite that, Americans' generation-long commitment to the stock market is being tested. In a *New York Times* article, Loren Fox, a senior analyst at Strategic Insight, a New York research and data firm, stated that "for a lot of ordinary people, the economic recovery does not feel real. People are not going to rush toward the stock market on a sustained basis until they feel more confident of employment growth and the sustainability of the economic recovery."[52]

Still, a lot of money is flowing into the stock market from small investors, pension funds, and other big institutional investors. However, according to Hewitt Associates, a consulting firm that tracks pension plans, many ordinary investors are reallocating their 401(k) retirement plans.[53] In the past, about three-quarters of 401(k) money was invested in stock funds. That's changing now. People are

---

52 Graham Bowley, "In Striking Shift, Small Investors Flee Stock Market," New York Times, August 21, 2010, www.nytimes.com/2010/08/22/business/22invest.html.
53 Ibid.

starting to invest their retirement money in other places as well as the stock market.

That could be a good thing, given all that we now know about the stock market. But it doesn't mean investors have stopped risking their money. Instead, they're like Las Vegas gamblers who decide to move from the roulette wheel (where the odds against their winning are huge) to the craps table (where the casino's "edge" is considerably less). In recent years, though, as Americans' sense of financial security has diminished, even stocks' reputation for being safe and profitable investments over time seems to have been dented as well.

For many investors, diversification appears to be the answer. They move their savings into a variety of vehicles, splitting it between equities and bonds, for example. This is a little like saying that if you play all the tables at a casino, the odds will be better that you'll win at least at some of them.

Bond fund sales benefited from this trend. Some of the investors who pulled their savings out of stocks put their money down on bond mutual funds instead. People who had become leery of the stock market sometimes took the profits they'd seen in the bullish stock market and invested them in bonds as a "safer" alternative.

When interest rates dropped, however, so did the yield from bonds. In 2008 the feds instituted a zero-interest-rate policy (ZIRP) to help stimulate the economy. Where a million dollars invested in ten-year Treasury bonds and left until maturity once gave a retiree about $45,000 a year in income, in today's world, that same $1 million yields only about $25,000. Some retirees who depended on their investments for income went back to taking on more risk in the hopes of maintaining their lifestyles.

Sometimes, risk pays off, but those times are usually the exceptions. In the long run, retirees who fall back on high-risk gambles for income are asking for trouble. This hasn't stopped many of them from gambling in ways they would never have considered before in the hopes of regaining the yields they once achieved from their more conservative investments. Many of the investors who had once relied on bonds now shifted their money into dividend-paying equities. Others went to high-yield bonds known as junk bonds. They're called junk for a reason! Investors in junk bonds face an assortment of new risks.

One type is interest-rate risk. When interest rates rise, the price of junk bonds drops. This type of risk is measured with a complicated formula that yields "duration": how much the value will bounce up and down as interest rates rise or fall. The higher the duration, the more "volatile" the bonds are considered to be. Volatility is a measurement that's calculated with another mathematical formula; it quantifies risk. An investment with a volatility of 50 percent, for example, would be considered to be very high risk because it has the potential to increase or decrease by as much as half its value. A bond that has a low coupon rate, a low yield to maturity, and a long term to maturity will have more volatility—and greater risk—than a bond with the opposite characteristics.

Another kind of risk investors face with junk bonds is default risk. The safest bonds (the ones with the least default risk) have a credit rating of AAA; junks bonds have ratings from C to BB. Default rates are usually higher during a recession and lower during stronger economic periods. Bonds that once seemed safe can become riskier as the economy changes. During 2008, for example, nearly half of the bonds with a C rating defaulted.

As interest rates increase, bond prices usually decrease, causing investors to chase after investment windfalls in yet another direction. Many of them reduce their bond holdings and make another shift to other forms of investment income, including dividend stocks.

Investors are hoping the dividends will replace lost retirement income, but their increased exposure to equity risk may cause them as many problems as if they'd kept their money in bonds.

Clearly, investors' love affair with risk has sent them running all over the investment playing field, constantly searching for the "game" that will yield the big win on which they've pinned their hopes for financial security. They seesaw back and forth between high-risk and low-risk options, always seeking the perfect gamble to give them the elusive jackpot winnings they're certain are out there.

THE PSYCHOLOGY OF RISK-TAKING

Financial advisors often ask their clients to assess their "tolerance for risk," as though the appropriate financial plan for each investor were only a matter of personality type. It's true that some people are more comfortable with more risk than others, but your comfort level will not make you any more or any less likely to win the jackpot.

Daniel Kahneman claims that the psychology of risk-taking is what clouds—not clarifies—people's financial decision making.[54] When it comes to financial decisions, Kahneman says, people can often be tricked (or trick themselves) into believing they are making the right investment choices because they base their acceptance of risk on rosy projections and hazy factors that have more to do with emotion and sentiment than they do with hard facts.

Traditional theory has always insisted that financial risk-taking is a purely cognitive activity. In other words, it's something that goes on inside our brains. Investors assume that when they shift their funds from stock to stock, from the stock market to bonds, or from bonds to equity dividends, they're making rational decisions. Neuroscientist

---

54 Daniel Kahneman, *Thinking Fast and Slow* (New York: Farrar, Straus and Giroux, 2011).

John Coates says his research indicates that investment decisions are based on factors that have very little do with intellectual analysis.[55] Many investors, for example, even intelligent and experienced ones, fail to understand the mathematics of risk. If you have a chain of four events, for example, each with a 90 percent chance of happening, most investors would take that to mean the overall risk is only 10 percent—when actually, it's 33 percent.

Every investor who makes financial decisions based on risk, says Coates, "succumbs to risk-taking behaviors that are cyclical . . . When things are going well, people take too much risk with worsening risk-reward trade-offs; when these bets blow up, people become risk averse." Investors' love-hate relationship with risk makes them bounce around the investment casino, from table to table. Alternatively, they follow the "buy-and-hold" strategy, which assumes that if they just wait long enough, their up-and-down risk levels will average out at an acceptable level. In other words, just keep playing the same table long enough, and you're bound to make out fine in the end. Meanwhile, investors who are preoccupied with managing risk levels often miss out on solid, stable financial opportunities.

Going to Las Vegas for a vacation is one thing. Turning it into a way of life is another. In the next chapter, we'd like to tell you about an investment alternative that makes a lot more sense.

FACT

You shouldn't be gambling with your hard-earned retirement money.

55 Kate Kelland, "John Coates, Former Wall Street Trader, Studies Neuroscience behind Financial Risk Taking," *Huffington Post*, December 10, 2012, www.huffingtonpost.com/2012/10/10/john-coates-wall-street-trader-neuroscientist_n_1953661.html.

CHAPTER 8

FACT OR FICTION:
FIXED-INDEX ANNUITIES HAVE AS MANY RISKS AND DRAWBACKS AS ANY OTHER FORM OF INVESTMENT

Human beings have a tendency to go to extremes. One day we're almost completely sedentary, spending most of our waking hours sitting in front of either a computer or a television, and the next day, driven by guilt, we launch an all-out exercise campaign. We yo-yo between eating junk food and eating nothing but salads. We go on spending sprees and then, to compensate, we try not to spend anything at all for the next few weeks. Our lives are pendulums, swinging back and forth, struggling to find a healthy equilibrium that seems to constantly elude us, no matter how many good resolutions we make.

Siddhartha Gautama, who would one day become known as the Buddha, started out his life as the pampered, totally sheltered son of a wealthy man. In reaction against his self-indulgent lifestyle, Siddhartha went to the opposite extreme: he practiced, as a way of life, a severe neglect of self. He left his father's palace and subjected himself to every extremity he could find: near nudity, extreme hunger, uncomfortable positions, burning heat, cold downpours. And then, one day, he was enlightened, and in the process, he realized that another option had presented itself to him: the "middle way," the path that leads between extremes.

When we think about retirement planning, we may feel as though our only options are the extreme ends of the investment spectrum: try to get rich quickly or go broke slowly. On the one end, we fall for the stock market's snake oil and give in blindly to our love affair with risk, and on the other end, we think CDs and money-market accounts are the only safe places to put our money. According to Bankrate.com, the average interest rate on a one-year CD is less than 1 percent.[56] This means that after you figure in both taxes and inflation, any money you stashed away in a CD is actually losing its purchasing power.

But there is another option. It's the plan B we mentioned back in chapter 3.

INVESTMENT'S "MIDDLE WAY"

An annuity is an investment contract between you and an insurance company. The initial investment is called the premium. Depending on the type of annuity, you earn different types of interest. This interest may be fixed—as it is, for example, in a CD or bond—or it

---

56 Bankrate, http://www.bankrate.com/cd.aspx.

may be variable—as it is, for example, in a mutual fund—or it may be a bit of both. A major feature of annuities is the ability to receive a guaranteed income for life. With some annuities, you can also receive gains from the market.

There are four types of annuities. One involves risk; the other three do not. Let's look at each one.

- *Variable annuity:* This is the only annuity that carries risk. A variable annuity is considered a security. This is because your purchase payment invests your money directly into the stock market—specifically, mutual funds. The investor reaps the gains when the market goes up but is also 100 percent exposed to the market downside, regardless of whether the market drops 5 percent or 50 percent. Since the performance of your annuity is based on mutual funds, a variable annuity carries the risk of principal loss in a down market. If the market value of your account drops, this will lead to lower payouts if you decide to annuitize your contract.

  Because variable annuities are securities, only a securities-licensed financial professional can sell them. Unlike most fixed or indexed annuities, a variable annuity is governed by FINRA.

- *Immediate annuity:* This is a series of payments guaranteed by an insurance company. The client invests a lump sum of money with the insurance company, and in turn, the insurance company guarantees a fixed amount of income for a certain period of time. The time frame may range from five years to life, with certain options to receive payments for either single or joint lives. Factors such as interest rates, life expectancy, and payment start date determine the amount of income paid out.

- *Fixed annuity:* Insurance companies sell fixed annuities. This type of annuity guarantees a fixed rate of return that may change annually or a multiyear rate that guarantees the same rate for the life of contract. Principal and any interest earned are guaranteed, similar to a certificate of deposit, although annuities are not guaranteed by any federal agency. As we mentioned earlier, there are also various annuitization provisions for guaranteed lifetime income.

- *Fixed-index or equity-index annuity:* This type of annuity has a unique feature: your money is not invested in the market, but you receive a credit based upon how the index performs. When that index goes up, you receive a good percentage of the gain. When the market drops, you never lose your principal or your gains. The major difference is that rather than a fixed rate of return, the interest credited is tied to the performance of an index such as the S&P 500. Unlike mutual funds, exchange-traded funds, or stocks, your principal is protected from market loss, and any interest earned is typically locked in on an annual basis, though that may vary from product to product. With a fixed-index annuity (FIA), insurance companies remove all the risk from your investment. In return, they take a portion of the upside in a growth market. You gain the ability to have an income at some point in the future without losing control of your principal now.

FIAs are protected against declines in the bond and equity markets. They offer a minimum guaranteed interest rate, with the potential for higher earnings than those offered by more traditional fixed annuities that are based on the performance of one or more stock-market indexes. Unlike bonds, if you were to purchase an FIA as part of your retirement plan, your earnings would grow tax-deferred. When a minimum guaranteed withdrawal benefit isn't already built into the FIA contract, you can pair it with an income rider that will give you the ability to activate a lifetime income stream during retirement.

FIXED-INDEX ANNUITY TERMINOLOGY

These terms will help you understand what we're talking about throughout this chapter:

- *Insurance company:* This is the company that issues the annuity. The insurance company backs the annuity's guarantees.

- *Contract owner and/or annuitant:* These are usually the same person, but they don't have to be. The owner makes decisions about the annuity, such as who the beneficiaries are. The annuitant is the person whose life expectancy is used to calculate annuity payments.

- *Beneficiary:* The beneficiary is the person who receives the annuity's death benefit. Naming one or more beneficiaries other than the estate is important because without a beneficiary, the money in your annuity could be subject to probate after your death.

- *Tax deferral:* Under current federal income tax law, any interest earned in your fixed-index annuity contract is tax-deferred. This means you won't have to pay ordinary income taxes on any taxable portion until you begin receiving money from your contract. If you take a withdrawal before retirement age (defined as fifty-nine and a half years), it will be taxed as ordinary income.

- *Cap:* Some FIAs set a maximum rate of interest (or cap) that the contract can earn in a specified period (usually a month or year). If the chosen index increase exceeds the cap, the cap will be used to calculate your interest. So, for example, if the annual cap were 3 percent and the value of the index rose by 4.8 percent, you would still only get 3 percent interest on your account. However, if the index change were 2.5 percent, that's the interest rate you'd get, since it's lower than your cap.

- *Spread:* The indexed interest for some annuities is determined by subtracting a percentage from any gain the index achieves in a specified period. For example, if the annuity has a 4 percent spread and the index increases 10 percent, the contract is credited 6 percent interest.

- *Participation rate:* In some annuities, a participation rate determines what percentage of the index increase is used to calculate your interest. In this case, let's suppose the index rose by 10 percent. If your cap is 12 percent, and your FIA has a 75 percent participation rate, you'll receive 7.5 percent in interest. (Participation rates are generally applied after caps and before a spread.)

HOW A FIXED-INDEX ANNUITY WORKS

Most fixed-index annuities have two phases: an accumulation phase, during which you let your money earn interest, and a distribution or payout phase, during which you receive money from your annuity. The accumulation phase begins as soon as you purchase your annuity. An FIA earns either a fixed rate of interest guaranteed by the insurance company or an interest rate based on the growth of an external index. Your principal and any bonuses are never subject to market-index risk. A downturn in the market index will never reduce your contract values! The distribution phase of an FIA begins whenever you choose to receive income payments. You can take income in the form of scheduled annuitization payments over your lifetime (or some other period of time). Many FIAs also allow you to take income withdrawals as an alternative to annuitization payments. In both cases, you can choose from several different payout options based on your personal needs.

Fixed-index annuities provide an opportunity for potential interest growth based on changes in one or more market indexes. Because of this potential, FIAs provide a unique opportunity for accumulation without risk, and since the interest is tax-deferred, it can accumulate your assets faster. (In addition to potential indexed interest, some FIAs also offer the option to receive fixed interest.)

If you can't shake an addiction to the stock market's risk adrenalin, then FIAs are definitely not for you! But if your goal is to ensure that you have income throughout your retirement, FIAs offer an unparalleled level of protection. This protection comes in three forms:

- *Accumulation:* Your principal and credited interest are protected against market downturns.

- *Guaranteed income:* You can be protected against the possibility of outliving your assets.

- *Death benefit:* If you die before annuity payments begin, a fixed-index annuity may help you provide for your loved ones.

There are two types of FIA: single premium, which is a one-time investment, and flexible premium, which allows for ongoing investments. With both kinds, you'll need to allocate your investment between a fixed account and one or more indexing strategies, giving you the best of both investment extremes. The fixed account will pay, for one or more years, a fixed rate of return that's usually higher than what a CD of the same length would give you, while the indexing strategies allow you to earn interest based on the stock market's performance during each year of the FIA contract. (Standard & Poor's 500 is the most common index used to measure the stock market's performance for FIAs, but others can be used as well.) If you diversify your investment among two or more FIAs, you may end up with a larger payoff.

Unlike a direct investment where you'd be suffering any losses caused by a drop in the stock market, if the index's return is negative, your investment doesn't lose anything. If the index's return is positive, however, you get interest on your account (up to a certain cap). This means you won't be participating in losses the way you would with other kinds of bond and equity investments. You also won't be gambling on hitting it big on the stock market, because of the cap on your FIA's interest. As we said, it's the middle way.

FIAs with income riders offer several advantages over other forms of investment:

- protection from market declines

- elimination of bond-default risk

- sustainable lifetime income

- simpler investment management

- no investment-management fees

FIAs do require a long-term commitment since their terms generally range from five to ten years, with longer terms also being available, which may include higher cap rates and premium bonuses. You'll have to pay a surrender charge if, during the FIA's term, you make annual withdrawals that are over a specified percentage of their investment value (typically, 10 percent).

FIAs have a stellar track record, but they should only be purchased from life insurance companies that have strong ratings from A.M. Best, Moody's, and Standard & Poors since income riders are only guaranteed subject to the insurance carrier's claims-paying ability.

An FIA offers real tax advantages. During the accumulation phase of your contract, all growth from interest is tax-deferred. If you were to purchase your FIA with after-tax dollars, when you begin withdrawing money, you'd only have to pay ordinary income taxes on your earnings and none on your premium payments. This tax-deferred growth, compounded over time, can increase the funds the FIA generated for your retirement.

You may be asking, "How is this better than a traditional IRA or 401(k), since these also allow me to defer taxes?" The answer is that FIAs don't have any government-imposed contribution limits, while

IRAs and 401(k)s do. If you have a flexible premium FIA, you can contribute as much money to it each year as you want to.

Tax deferral can be a powerful retirement strategy. Suppose, for example, that you put an initial $100,000 into an FIA that compounded at 4 percent annually with all taxes deferred. Twenty years later, after taxes are paid on the lump-sum distribution, the amount would be thousands of dollars greater than if you had put the same amount in a taxable investment. Of course, if you were to purchase an annuity using funds from an account that already provides tax deferral, you wouldn't get any additional tax benefit. But there are still strong incentives for choosing an FIA.

Another advantage of an FIA is the opportunity to accumulate interest based on changes in an external index; some FIAs allow you to spread your investment across more than one index. In that case, you can decide what portion of your annuity's value you want, based on each index you've chosen. If this sounds overwhelming or confusing, let us refer you back to chapter 1: you need a trusted advisor who can guide you through these decisions. Keep in mind, though, that it's hard to go too far wrong with FIAs: although an external-market index or indexes can affect your contract values, you're not buying shares of any stock or index fund. The contract does not directly participate in any stock or equity or bond investments, so whatever indexes you choose, you're never going to lose money.

At the end of each contract year, your interest is calculated based on the selected market index or indexes. If the result is a positive number, you will automatically receive indexed interest (subject to a participation rate and a cap or spread, which we'll explain further later). The interest is locked in each year; it can never be lost due to future year's index declines. What happens if the result is negative? Nothing. If you're a risk junky, that answer might sound pretty disappointing, but it's actually good news. You won't receive any additional interest for that year—but your annuity's value won't decline either, because there's an annual reset.

In other words, at the end of each contract year, your annuity's index values are automatically reset: this year's ending value becomes next year's starting value. Annual reset also locks in any interest your contract earned during the year. This means that if the index drops, your contract value will hold steady. Then, when the market index rises, you don't have to make up any previous losses before your annuity can start earning interest again. Thanks to annual reset, your accumulation value will increase during any year in which the market index goes up.

You also have the option to choose the crediting method your FIA uses. (Again, don't hesitate to seek advice from an advisor you can trust to have your best interests as the priority.) No single crediting method consistently delivers the most interest under all market conditions.

FIA STRATEGY OPTIONS

Given today's interest rates, the FIA industry has shifted dramatically from capped products to uncapped products. When most products showed annual caps less than 3.5 percent (and some less than 3 percent), it was difficult to present a growth opportunity with those limits. The answer was to present strategies that don't cap growth, and the industry has adopted quite a number of different strategies to achieve this. Along with this has come the implementation of managed-proprietary indexes, many of which are designed to minimize volatility and provide smoother and more consistent positive results. Options based on the traditional unmanaged S&P 500 index still exist.

A volatility-controlled index is a way to manage fluctuations experienced in an underlying index such as the S&P 500. These indexes usually have two components: an underlying index and a stable asset, usually cash. Their structure allows them to continuously balance assets between the index and cash, based on measured market volatility, in order to keep the overall amount of risk (as measured by volatility) at a fairly steady level. Avoiding the big swings that might otherwise happen during a volatile market phase gives more stable, predictable returns. Your returns might not be as high over time as the "pure" index, but the added stability of a volatility-controlled index can be a big benefit to you.

Because volatility is the primary factor in hedging costs, a relatively stable hedging price means that when it comes time for renewal, insurers can offer more stable spreads, participation rates, and caps. When returns are more stable, this also means the insurer is less likely to have to pay out on underlying guarantees when markets perform poorly. Reducing this risk is good for everybody. It allows for higher caps and participation rates or lower spreads.

Another type of indexed crediting strategy involves the use of alternative indices.

We need to look at the various options to understand which strategies provide the best growth opportunity. Results can be deceiving.

- *Annual point-to-point with spread:* This is the most direct crediting method, where the index is viewed on the first day of the contract year and the last day of the contract year. The spread represents the amount of gain retained by the company. For example, a 10 percent index gain with a .75 percent spread would result in a gain for the client of 9.25 percent. When considering FIAs with this crediting method, look carefully at spreads, as they can vary from a low of .75 percent to a high of over 3 percent.

- *Annual point-to-point with participation rate:* In this method, the client is credited with a percentage of that annual gain in the index. For example, a 10 percent index gain with a 50 percent participation rate would result in a 5 percent gain for the client.

- *Annual point-to-point with a cap:* With this crediting method, the client is credited with all of the gains in the index up to a stated cap, or limit. For example, a 10 percent index gain with a 3.5 percent cap would result in a 3.5 percent gain for the client.

- *Multiyear crediting:* Some products offer higher participation rates and lower spreads if the interest-crediting period is longer than one year. There are products offering periods as long as five years, though many more offer two- and three-year periods. This strategy can result in higher gains, but it can also result in longer periods of zero growth. These strategies are best suited to younger clients and those who do not plan to take account withdrawals for at least five to ten years.

- *Proprietary-managed indexes:* This latest development in the industry uses proprietary indexes instead of the traditional S&P 500, DJIA, and NASDAQ. Barclays, Merrill Lynch, BlackRock, and Morgan Stanley are a few of the companies participating. They don't issue the products, and the client's money is not invested in the index; it is simply used to determine the interest credits. Most of these indexes are managed to limit volatility, and therefore, their performance will be consistent, but they tend not to have large gains in strong bull markets.

- *S&P 500:* This unmanaged index of five hundred stocks is still the most stalwart of the industry. It is, perhaps, the best indicator of overall market performance, and many products offer a variety of interest crediting strategies based on this single index.

THE IMPACT OF NO LOSSES

We can't emphasize enough how important it is to avoid any losses in calculating long-term growth—and the FIA product is specifically designed to do that. Your initial reaction to getting "only" 50 percent of the gains or having the company keep the first 2 percent of gains through a spread should be tempered by the reality that when the index is down (for example, by more than 40 percent, as it was in 2008), you won't lose a penny—*and* when the next contract year starts, the index starts at that lower figure.

THE IMPACT OF LARGE GAINS

Here is where the uncapped products shine and why one must look closely at available index options. A 50 percent participation rate only returns 2.5 percent when the index is up 5 percent, but it returns to 15 percent when the index is up 30 percent. Long-term gains in the market have always been fueled by those periodic large gains, and utilizing a participation-rate strategy capitalizes on that. The same applies to a spread strategy. A 2 percent spread with a 5 percent index gain results in a 3 percent gain for the client, but the same spread with a 30 percent gain results in 28 percent to the client.

The key is to match the strategy with the index. The S&P 500 index provides the highest "up" years, but spreads tend to be higher and the participation rates tend to be lower. The higher participation rates and lower spreads tend to be associated with the managed-proprietary indexes that have smaller "ups."

We have included performance histories of several different uncapped strategies utilizing both the S&P 500 index and a proprietary index.

THE IMPACT OF UNCAPPED PARTICIPATION RATE ON THE S&P 500 INDEX WITH 50 PERCENT PARTICIPATION RATE

Year	S&P 500	50% Participation
2006	12.62%	6.31%
2007	4.34%	2.17%
2008	−40.67%	0
2009	26.53%	13.26%
2010	11.81%	5.90%
2011	0.14%	.07%
2012	14.39%	7.20%
2013	27.10%	13.55%
2014	13.63%	6.81%
2015	-0.01%	0
Total	69.89%	55.27
Average	6.989%	5.527%

THE IMPACT OF UNCAPPED PARTICIPATION RATE ON THE
S&P 500 INDEX WITH 40 PERCENT PARTICIPATION RATE

Year	S&P 500	40% Participation
2006	12.62%	5.04%
2007	4.34%	1.73%
2008	−40.67%	0
2009	26.53%	10.61%
2010	11.81%	4.72%
2011	0.14%	.04%
2012	14.39%	5.75%
2013	27.10%	10.84%
2014	13.63%	5.45%
2015	−0.01%	0
Total	69.89%	44.18
Average	6.989%	4.418%

PROPRIETARY INDEX (S&P 500 DIVIDEND ARISTOCRATS
DAILY RISK CONTROL 5% INDEX) WITH .75% SPREAD

Year	Aristocrats	Return
2006	11.49%	10.74%
2007	3.65%	2.90%
2008	0.25%	0
2009	6.81%	6.06%
2010	6.83%	6.08%
2011	0.82%	.07%
2012	5.87%	5.12%
2013	13.13%	12.38%
2014	5.17%	4.42%
2015	−1.10%	0
Total	52.92%	47.77
Average	5.292%	4.777%

Here's what our analysis tells us: the best long-term growth opportunity is provided by a high participation rate or low spread based on the S&P 500. Through those you can earn as much as 92 percent of the index gains without ever experiencing a loss in a down market.

An alternative index can also include euro or emerging markets, specific industry sectors, commodities, or any of a variety of other measures of economic performance. The variety of alternative offerings is still expanding, but they all share one thing in common: although it's possible to receive zero interest credits, you will never receive less than zero. Each strategy can offer that guarantee because it limits upside potential in some manner. Talk to an expert to decide which strategy will work best for you.

BUILDING YOUR FUTURE INCOME

We want to repeat: FIAs take away the risk that's inherent in other forms of investment. All the risk has been transferred to the insurance company that issues the FIA. This guarantee protects your assets, your retirement income, and your beneficiaries. A fixed-index annuity puts you in control of your future income, based on the annuity you choose and how much money you put into it.

After your contract has had an opportunity to earn interest over its accumulation period, you can begin distribution. As long as you abide by the terms of your contract, you will not lose any of the money you place in your annuity due to surrender charges. Annuities are subject to surrender charge periods, which can vary, but are generally between five and ten years. Once that period is up, you can then receive the FIA's value in a stream of income that will last your lifetime (or longer).

The amount of your payments will be based on the payout schedule you choose, as well as the FIA's value on the date you begin distribution. With most FIAs, you have two options for receiving income payments: annuitization payments or income withdrawals. You can schedule your income payments as withdrawals that begin any time after you reach a certain age (often age sixty). In some cases, your income payments will be larger if you postpone taking them for a few years.

For annuities that are not held in a qualified plan such as an IRA or a 401(k), part of each annuitization payment is a tax-free return of what you paid for the annuity, and part is taxable as interest you earned on the annuity. Income withdrawals under the same annuity are fully taxable until the interest you earned has been withdrawn. After that, you withdraw what you paid for the annuity tax-free. (Talk to your tax advisor before choosing between annuitization payments and income withdrawals.)

We've already told you that an FIA allows you to convert your annuity's value into a series of fixed-amount payments that will last for your lifetime—but that's not the end of the good news. Depending on the product you choose, many FIAs also offer optional income riders with payments that can increase. This allows you to compensate for inflation throughout retirement. This is an obvious benefit, but you'll have to pay for it. These riders have to be purchased at a cost above your normal FIA contributions.

FIAs also have inheritance benefits. Say you were to die before you began to receive your annuity's payouts. In that case, your beneficiary would receive a death benefit. In some cases, even if you were to die after you started receiving FIA income, your beneficiary could receive a death benefit. Your beneficiary could choose to receive your contract's values as a single payment or as a series of payments over time.

When FIAs have so many advantages, why aren't more people using them for retirement planning? That's a good question. One answer is that since brokers don't get the kickback they would receive from a mutual fund or other form of investment, financial advisors aren't motivated to tell their clients about them. There are also a lot of FIA myths circulating out there.

FIXED-INDEX ANNUITIES MYTHS

MYTH #1:
ALL ANNUITY FEES ARE HIGH.

Reality: Variable annuity fees are indeed high and can average 5 percent (and some go as high as 8 percent if you purchase many riders) of your account's annual balance. This is not too different from many mutual funds or managed-money funds, where the fees, typically, are around 2 to 3 percent per year. However, fixed annuities and FIAs have very low or no annual fees, far less than the typical mutual fund.

MYTH #2:
THERE ARE BIG COMMISSIONS IN ANNUITIES.

Reality: The commissions paid on fixed or fixed-index annuities do *not* come from the investor's funds. Often, a bonus of 5 to 10 percent is added to the investors' original balance. This is very different from "load" mutual funds, where the commission is subtracted from the investor's funds.

Here's an example: if an investor invests $100,000 in a fixed-index annuity, he could have $105,000 to $110,000 working for him on day one. In contrast, $100,000 invested in a mutual fund with a 5 percent "load" would give the investor a market value of $95,000 on day one. Additionally, the mutual-fund investor could incur annual fees of 2 to 3 percent. In fact, over the last ten years, owners of mutual funds or managed-money funds have paid up to 35 percent in total fees, even though they have lost 20 to 40 percent of their principal due to market corrections. In contrast, the purchaser of the fixed-index annuity would have paid *no* fees, and *no* commissions would have been subtracted from his original investment.

MYTH #3:
I CAN'T BUY AN ANNUITY, BECAUSE SURRENDER PENALTIES PREVENT ME GETTING MY MONEY OUT FOR TEN TO FIFTEEN YEARS.

Reality: Annuities come in all sorts of durations, from one to twenty years. If you pull money out early, yes, there may be a surrender penalty, but over time, the surrender penalties decrease and eventually cease. This is very different from bank CDs, where it's all or nothing. If you were to purchase a five-year bank CD and then pulled your money out a month early (at month fifty-nine), you'd suffer the same "early withdrawal penalty" on *all* your money. *Most fixed-index annuities allow you to withdraw 10 percent of your money each year without a penalty.*

Surrender penalties can actually be good for the long-term annuity purchaser. It allows the insurance company to give a 5 to 10 percent bonus up front, or a higher interest rate, knowing that it will have the funds for many years. An analogy is the 10 percent IRS penalty on people who withdraw funds from their traditional IRA or 401(k) prior to age fifty-nine and a half. This is actually a good deterrent to people robbing their retirement account.

MYTH #4:
ANNUITIES ARE ONLY FOR OLD PEOPLE.

Reality: The average age at which owners purchase their first annuity is fifty-two. However, millions of teachers have contributed to annuities, starting as early as in their twenties. The real issue should be whether investors want to risk losing 20 to 50 percent of their life savings whenever the stock and bond markets have a correction or whether they prefer the safety of an FIA.

MYTH #5:
BECAUSE AN INVESTOR'S EARNINGS ARE TAX-DEFERRED INSIDE AN ANNUITY, IT MAKES NO SENSE TO PURCHASE AN ANNUITY INSIDE A TRADITIONAL IRA OR 401(K) OR OTHER QUALIFIED RETIREMENT ACCOUNT.

Reality: This is a common perception often held by many CPAs. However, fixed or fixed-index annuities can often yield a higher interest rate than bank CDs and are guaranteed to have no principal lost. Why should the CPA's clients not want to protect their life savings?

FIXED-INDEX ANNUITY FACTS

When we start talking to our clients about fixed-rate annuities, they usually ask us several questions.

We're going to give you our answers here, right now:

1.   *Can I lose money?*

     No. Fixed-index, fixed, and immediate annuities are guaranteed by the insurance companies that issue the contracts. Your principal is protected by the claims-paying ability of those companies. Of course, excess withdrawals may result in surrender charges, and if you are under fifty-nine and a half years old and you make withdrawals, you will be subject to additional tax penalties.

2. *Do I pay high fees every year?*

No. Unlike variable annuities, which have an investment feature (and have fees that can get as high as 8 percent each year, in our experience), the annuities we promote either do not have any fees for the base contract or have very low fees for additional riders you may choose (such as spousal continuation, inflation protection, death benefit, lifetime income, etc.)—and those fees are, typically, less than 1 percent each.

3. *Will my cash flow fluctuate?*

No. Fluctuating means your income can swing up and swing down from month to month, or year to year, however you have it set up. With the annuity strategies we recommend, your income can only go up and up to provide a hedge against inflation. FIAs can go up due to index-linked interest rates, and they go up for every year you wait or don't turn on income. You can be assured that your cash flow will not decrease. And that is income that you and or your spouse will not outlive!

4. *Will we be able to keep our money if one of us becomes ill or passes away?*

Yes. There are many annuities or additional riders that have waivers for terminally ill or premature death situations. There are annuities that may provide double or even triple your income for qualifying health-care expenses. Many annuities or additional riders offer death-benefit provisions as well. A well-researched annuity strategy designed for your specific needs and goals is the best way to go.

5. *Can these annuities provide me with income for the rest of my life?*

Yes. With an FIA, you can select the option to purchase a lifetime-income contract. Some are structured that way, some add this feature through a rider for an additional cost, but yes, the annuities we work with and strategies we design offer an income-for-life benefit.

6. *Does my income have the potential to grow to keep up with inflation?*

Yes. This is something people often don't think about, but we do. In our annuity strategies, we leverage annuity features and riders to help ensure our clients' incomes grow as the cost of living increases. We want you to retain the purchasing power of your money.

7. *Will I completely lose access to all my money?*

No. You do not have to annuitize. You want to make sure you select the right annuity type and features for your own unique situation, but many offer up to a 10 percent annual withdrawal without penalty. (As long as you're over fifty-nine and a half. Otherwise, you incur a tax penalty.) You do have the ability to get more (or all), but you'll pay a surrender charge. (Please note that the annuity you purchase will probably have a penalty period for the first three to fifteen years, with a sequentially decreasing percent charged against your withdrawal funds for excess withdrawals or full surrender of the contract. So you should not purchase an annuity with money you think you may need in the near term.)

8. *Can I get even more income by "laddering" annuities?*

Yes. Often, with well-planned-out annuity strategies and payout-management techniques, using more than one annuity for income—engaged at specific points in time— can net most people higher monthly and annual payouts.

9. *Does anything protect me against the risk that the insurance company might go under, causing me to lose my investment?*

Yes. All companies that are licensed to sell annuities must be members of the state's guaranty association, which protects consumers in case the insurer becomes insolvent. If an insurer starts to have financial trouble, the insurance regulator in its home state works with the guaranty association to find another company to take over its business. If regulators can't find another insurer, then the guaranty association coverage kicks in. All states cover at least $250,000 in annuity benefits, and twelve states, as well as the District of Columbia, have limits of $300,000 or more. For added peace of mind, look for a company with a financial strength rating of B+ or higher from A.M. Best, and to be completely safe, split your annuity investments between two or more insurers if that will keep you below the coverage limits. Even in a worst-case scenario, though, the risks are low. Insurance companies don't go under very often. In fact, only a very few small insurers that sell annuities have ever gone broke.

FIA'S BOTTOM LINE

Today's FIA products are designed to be used for specific purposes, as evidenced by the myriad options in income riders, death-benefit riders, index options, and crediting methods. Embarking on an Internet search for information so you can decide for yourself the best option is an open invitation to make the wrong choice. It only makes sense to talk to a professional who can explain the various options to you and help you learn how those options can be best put to work to meet your specific needs.

Mark Twain once said, "I am more concerned with the *return of* my money than the *return on* my money." The thing to remember about FIAs is this: you will never lose a penny of principal, and your investment will gain even when the market drops. Annuities aren't intended to give you amazing investment growth; they lack the gambler's thrill of big risks with the elusive potential of high payoffs. Instead, they're a way to "return" your money to you in such a way that you can live your life during retirement the way you want, with the peace of mind of knowing that you will never outlive that income. They're a stable, secure middle way. The Buddha would approve.

FACT
With fixed-index annuities, you never lose your money.

CHAPTER 9

FACT OR FICTION:
IT'S TOO LATE TO SIGNIFICANTLY
CHANGE MY RETIREMENT PLAN

When you were a student, were you one of those disciplined young people who began studying for a final exam weeks in advance? Or did you leave it until the last minute and stay up all night cramming the night before the exam? There's a lot to be said for the first approach as the better option. But what if you went for a third option and didn't study at all? What if, the day before the exam, you told yourself, "Since I didn't study ahead of time, there's no point in me studying now"? Instead of using the time you have, you say, "I might as well forget all about studying and do the best I can without it. Tonight I'll just party for a while and then go to bed." That approach is the worst choice out of the three!

Obviously, the longer you prepare for an exam, the better off you are likely to be, but even some studying is better than no studying. That last-minute cram session could very well make the difference between passing and failing your exam.

The same approach is true for retirement planning. Ideally, you should start an effective retirement plan as early as possible in your working life. But if you don't—and many people don't—you're better off doing what you can now, as soon as possible, rather than just giving up on having a well-planned retirement strategy.

We've all heard the phrase "better late than never." We sometimes use it about others' efforts with a tone of grudging acceptance or exasperation. But this truism often has real truth. "Better late than never" means a situation that needed to be resolved has been resolved; it means that work that was delayed (perhaps for legitimate reasons) has now been delivered. Something is now being addressed that may have not gotten the attention it required earlier, due to lack of time, money, or maturity. Loose ends are tied up so that your hopes can be fulfilled.

If you've put off creating a retirement strategy, "better late than never" applies to you! None of us can undo the past; we cannot go back and undo what we did, nor can we do what we didn't do. But as the great financier J. P. Morgan said, "The first step toward getting somewhere is to decide you're not going to stay where you are." After you take that first step, there are further practical steps you can take now that will make a difference to your future.

BETTER-LATE-THAN-NEVER RETIREMENT STRATEGIES

We're going to go back to what we told you in the first chapter and say it again: first and foremost, you need a trusted advisor who can point you toward the retirement strategies that will be best for you, no matter your age or circumstances. Remember that trying to go it alone when it comes to retirement planning is about as sensible as trying to give yourself a root canal! The longer you've waited to begin, the more you're going to need an expert's advice.

Here are some of the strategies you should discuss with your retirement advisor:

- Move at least some of your investments into FIAs that could guarantee you a fixed income in as little as five years.

- Once you have a guaranteed income stream, you can build your plans for your retirement lifestyle around that. You'll be able to plan what you can afford and what you can't. Think about what you truly need to be happy.

- Work as long as you can. This means taking care of your health, starting today. Besides providing you with both additional income and more time to save, working will also keep you active, which is good for your physical and mental health. The longer you work, even if it's just a little, will help delay the need to tap into your retirement savings, pensions, and Social Security. You can also decide when to retire based on when your FIA income can begin at the best level possible.

- Get the most out of Social Security.

STRATEGIES FOR MAXIMIZING SOCIAL SECURITY

Let's talk in more detail about how to maximize your Social Security. You can take benefits early, when you're sixty-two (earlier if you are a survivor or on disability), or you can wait as late as seventy. By taking benefits earlier rather than later, you could end up collecting a lot less over the course of your lifetime.

Full retirement age (also known as normal retirement age, or NRA) is when you're eligible to receive full Social Security benefits. The full retirement age used to be sixty-five for everyone, but that's changed now, as you can see by looking at the table.

RETIREMENT AGES FOR FULL SOCIAL SECURITY BENEFITS

Year You Were Born	Your Full Retirement Age
1942	65 and 10 months
1943-1954	66
1955	66 and 2 months
1956	66 and 4 months
1957	66 and 6 months
1958	66 and 8 months
1959	66 and 10 months
1960 or later	67

If you decide to take Social Security payments before your full retirement age, you might get more years of Social Security benefits, but you might also get less money over the course of your lifetime. People who start receiving their Social Security check up to thirty-six months before their full retirement age will have their benefits permanently reduced by five-ninths of 1 percent for each month. Those who go on Social Security benefits *more* than thirty-six months before their full retirement age will have their benefits further reduced by five-twelfths of 1 percent per month.

That may not sound like all that much, but when you do the math, you'll see how it adds up. If your full retirement age is sixty-six, for example, and you start your Social Security benefits when you're sixty-two, the reduced-benefit calculation will be based on forty-eight months. The reduction for the first thirty-six months is actually 20 percent (five-ninths of 1 percent times thirty-six), and then you'll lose 5 percent (five-twelfths of 1 percent times twelve) for the remaining twelve months. Your total permanent benefits would be reduced by 25 percent.

It works the other way around—to your benefit—when you delay Social Security payments. Every year that you delay claiming benefits, between the ages of sixty-two and seventy, your payments rise about 7 or 8 percent (and that's before inflation adjustments). If you're married, you and your spouse might be able to ramp up your potential lifetime benefits even more. For example, let's say you are sixty-two, with an annual salary of $100,000, while your spouse makes $60,000 a year. If you both take Social Security benefits at sixty-two, you might collect $1.1 million or so in lifetime benefits (according to Financial Engines' Social Security calculator). But if, instead, your spouse starts Social Security benefits at sixty-four while you file for your own benefits to start when you're seventy, with a "restricted application" when you're sixty-six that allows you to take spousal benefits, you could increase the amount of Social Security income you and your spouse collect over your joint lifetimes by almost $300,000.

Here again, given the money at stake and the complexity of the Social Security system, you need to talk to your trusted financial advisor to determine the best Social Security strategy for your circumstances. Here are some factors to talk over with your advisor as you make your Social Security decisions:

- *Your cash needs:* If you have other sources of income (an FIA, for example, or a traditional pension), your Social Security benefits will make up a smaller fraction of your total retirement strategy. This means you might be able to afford to be more flexible about when you take Social Security benefits. If you'll need your Social Security benefits to make ends meet, however, you'll probably want to delay Social Security income as long as your health and other circumstances allow so that you can maximize your benefits.

- *Your life expectancy and break-even age:* You've seen that taking Social Security benefits early reduces your monthly benefits, but of course it also means you could receive monthly checks for a longer time. On the other hand, taking Social Security benefits later results in fewer checks during your lifetime, but the credit for waiting means each check will be larger. Your break-even age will depend on several factors, including the amount of your benefits, the taxes you'll need to pay on that amount, and the cost of missed opportunities (such as other investments you could have made). If you have an average to above-average life expectancy, then it probably makes sense for you to delay retiring as long as you can. If you're in poor health or have reason to think you'll die younger than the average life expectancy, however, you might what to take what you can get while you can.

While we're talking about life expectancy, this might be a good time to explain that according to the National Center for Health Statistics, our average life expectancy at birth is about seventy-nine years (if you're a man, it's a little less than that, and if you're a woman, it's a little more). Once you turn sixty-five, though, your average life expectancy goes up to eighty-two for men and eighty-five for women, with the average even higher for married couples. If you and your spouse both live to be sixty-five years old, you have a more than 60 percent chance of living to be ninety or older.[57] Remember these are only *averages*. You could very well live to a younger age—or an older one. You'll need to consider your own personal life expectancy, taking into consideration factors such as your health, your family history, and your lifestyle.

This table gives Social Security's 2015 numbers for break-even ages. (It doesn't include any adjustments for inflation or missed investment opportunities.)

Monthly Social Security Benefits	Retirement Age	Break-Even Age
$2,025	62 vs. 66	Between 77 and 78
$2,713	62 vs. 70	Between 80 and 81
$3,606	66 vs. 70	Between 82 and 83

- *Your spouse:* When you make a decision about when to receive Social Security, you'll need to also take into account your spouse's age and health, particularly if you're the higher-earning spouse. If you didn't earn much during

57 National Center for Health Statistics, http://www.cdc.gov/nchs.

your working years, but your spouse did, you could get more Social Security income when your spouse dies; the greater the higher-earning spouse's benefit, the better for the surviving spouse. The Social Security Administration offers several strategies for married couples, which you should discuss with your retirement planner.

- *Whether you're still working:* Earning wages (including self-employment income) could reduce your benefit temporarily if you take Social Security benefits early. If you haven't reached your full retirement age, for example, and you're still working, one dollar in benefits will be deducted for every two dollars you earn above the annual limit (which, in 2015, was $15,720). Starting the month you hit your full retirement age, though, your benefits are no longer reduced no matter how much you earn. However, during the months *before* your birthday of that year, your deductions will be one dollar for every three dollars you earn above a higher limit (which was $41,880 in 2015).[58] In a sense, though, you will get these deductions back in the form of a higher benefit at full retirement age, so you may not want to cut back on working just because you're worried you'll earn too much. However, keep in mind that Social Security benefits are taxable, so if your taxable income becomes higher because of work income, you could lose more of your Social Security income to taxes.

What if you've already started collecting Social Security, and now, with new information, you want to change your mind? You

---

58 Social Security Administration, https://www.ssa.gov.

can do that so long as it's been a year or less since you went on Social Security benefits. You'll have to pay the government back the money you've already received, but think of it as buying an annuity that will allow you to increase your retirement income. You'll have to come up with the repayment money, but you won't have to pay interest on the benefits you already receive, and there are no fees to pay.

Some people believe that the future of Social Security is so shaky that they should begin collecting benefits as soon as they can. They want to grab what they can while they can. If you have these concerns, talk them over with your financial advisor. Most people will find that it's usually in their best interest to wait as long as they can (but no later than age seventy) to start collecting Social Security benefits.

INSURING THE FUTURE

Obviously, no insurance in the world can protect us from accidents and illness and eventual death. It can, however, protect us and the people we love from the financial consequences of these events. Insurance is intended to protect us against a possible future event that could be financially catastrophic. We buy car insurance to protect ourselves against the cost of an accident; we buy medical insurance to protect ourselves against the cost of health-care expenses; we may buy life insurance to protect our children or spouse from the loss of income our premature death might cause.

If an unpredictable event won't cause a financial catastrophe, then insurance probably isn't necessary. For example, losing a cell phone can be annoying, but it's not catastrophic. And if you have enough financial resources to recover from what might otherwise be catastrophic, you can "self-insure." Multimillionaires probably don't need life insurance because if they were to die unexpectedly, their family would inherit a financial legacy.

INSURING YOUR RETIREMENT

The need for "retirement insurance" is a little more difficult to determine. You should consider several possible unpredictable future events:

- *How long you'll live:* Even if you formally calculate your life expectancy, it's just an estimate. You can easily live many years beyond your predicted life expectancy—or you could die prematurely.

- *Future inflation that increases your living expenses.*

- *Your financial discipline:* Can you resist the temptation to use retirement savings for more immediate needs or desires?

The combined financial consequences of these factors could be that you outlive your money. You may find that your retirement income no longer covers your living expenses. Insuring your retirement income means making certain you'll have income streams that will:

- last the rest of your life, no matter how long you live

- enable you to survive a stock-market crisis, no matter how serious

- still cover your living expenses, even if inflation pushes them higher

- be paid automatically without any effort or actions on your part

Only three sources of retirement income meet most or all of these criteria. Social Security meets all the criteria, which is why you should maximize your Social Security income as a form of retirement insurance. The old-fashioned employer-provided pensions met most of the criteria, although they didn't usually increase to account for inflation. As we've explained in an earlier chapter, these pensions are no longer the secure thing they once were. And last, annuities bought from an insurance company automatically provide you a monthly paycheck for the rest of your life, and they won't be affected by stock-market crashes. Some annuities are fixed, which means they are still vulnerable to inflation, while others increase for inflation or increase at a fixed rate, such as 3 percent per year. Annuities give you retirement insurance.

LIFE INSURANCE

If you're concerned about leaving something behind for your heirs (and you're not a multimillionaire), you might want to consider a life insurance policy. You could pay the premiums using other retirement-fund vehicles.

For instance, if you have a traditional IRA, starting when you reach seventy and a half, you'll be required to take out a minimum amount of money every year. If you've already insured your own retirement income through an annuity, you could use your required minimum distributions from your IRA to pay premiums on a life insurance policy with a guaranteed death benefit. That way, your heirs will inherit life insurance proceeds free of income tax. If your estate is large enough that federal estate tax will take a chunk out of it, with the proper planning, the insurance proceeds can avoid that tax as well. When you hold the life insurance in a trust, the proceeds won't count toward the federal estate-tax exemption (which in 2015 was $5.43 million or $10.86 million for a couple).[59] Residents in states with lower exemptions than the federal threshold could benefit from the strategy.

A universal or whole-life policy, which builds up cash value, is usually the best choice when your goal is to leave money to your heirs. These types of policy are more expensive than a term policy, which expires after a certain period. Your age and health factor into the premium costs, as will the amount of the death benefit you want, and then you'll need to decide if you can afford the cost of this insurance. To give you some idea of what to expect, a seventy-year-old man who is considered a standard risk (in other words, he has no serious health conditions) and who wants a policy with a $1 million death benefit would have to pay about $40,000 a year in life insurance premiums.

This strategy isn't for everyone. You must consider whether you'll need the money you'll spend on premiums for things such as unexpected medical bills. You might want to also consider investing instead of buying insurance. The same seventy-year-old man might get a larger payoff by investing his $40,000 every year. If he lives to be eighty-eight, and he gets a 5 percent annual return, he'll have about $1.2 million to leave to his heirs. They'll only owe income or capital-gains tax on appreciation *after* the date of his death.

---

59 Ibid.

LONG-TERM-CARE INSURANCE

Another step you can take now to insure your retirement years and protect your family against future expenses is to consider options for providing for your future health needs. Although you may not want to think about it, most of us will, eventually, need some sort of long-term health care. In fact, according to the US Department of Health and Human Services, 70 percent of all people turning sixty-five are going to need it before they die. It makes sense to plan ahead now, while you still have your health!

Long-term-care insurance could be a part of that plan. Even though it's expensive (policies typically range between $3,000 and $6,000 a year, depending on a variety of factors, such as sex, age, health status, maximum daily benefit, length of benefit, and waiting period), it's an investment that could pay off. To make a long-term-care claim, you need to be unable to perform at least two "activities of daily living," such as bathing, dressing, feeding, and toileting. When you can't do these ordinary things, you're likely to end up in a nursing home, and just one year there could cost you or your family nearly $90,000. Some regions of the country, such as New York City, have even higher costs. Meanwhile, the average cost of care is increasing by more than 4 percent a year.[60]

Costs such as these could easily eat up all or more than your monthly retirement income. They could also swallow the assets you're hoping to leave to your spouse or your children when you die. Long-term-care insurance would reimburse you for these costs. That expensive policy no longer seems quite so expensive when you

---

60 Emily Mullin, "How to Pay for Nursing Home Costs," US News & World Report, http://health.usnews.com/health-news/best-nursing-homes/articles/2013/02/26/how-to-pay-for-nursing-home-costs.

consider that the annual premium might be far less than what you'd end up paying for a one-month stay in a nursing home.

There are ways you can get more out of long-term-care insurance premiums. The best way is to buy the insurance as early as you can and while you're still in good health. But remember that "better late than never" applies here too! If you wait until you're seventy to buy long-term-care insurance, you could pay as much as three times what you would have if you'd bought it when you were fifty. But even those higher premiums will pay off in a month or two if you end up needing to go into a nursing home. You're also unlikely to have made the payments for as many years before you'll need the coverage, so if you're older, you might want to pull the cost of premiums from another already-existing savings fund. Keep in mind, though, that rates for long-term-care insurance are a little like health insurance: they tend to go up. The younger you are when you start, the lower the base number upon which any future increases will be determined. The most important thing is to purchase long-term-care insurance *before* you need it.

The traditional version of long-term-care insurance works a little like both health-care insurance and car insurance: you pay a monthly, quarterly, or annual premium to the insurance company, and in return, the company limits your exposure to asset risk. If you never get sick or you never have an accident, the insurance companies don't refund your premiums, of course, so this means that you're paying for something you hope you'll never have to use. You do that because you know that a single hospitalization or car accident could cost you far more than several years' worth of insurance premiums. But what if your heirs could get back the money you spent on long-term-care insurance if you were not to use it?

COMBINING LONG-TERM-CARE INSURANCE WITH LIFE INSURANCE

With some hybrid versions of long-term-care insurance, if you don't use it, you don't really lose it, because these hybrids combine life insurance with long-term-care insurance. Ordinarily, you would purchase long-term-care insurance and life insurance separately. Life insurance pays a death benefit to your beneficiaries when you die; permanent life insurance policies allow you to accumulate cash value within the policy, which you can eventually borrow against or use to pay premiums. Long-term-care insurance, on the other hand, defrays costs if you spend time in a long-term-care facility or need in-home help. A hybrid policy combines the two so that your benefits can be used either for long-term care or life insurance—or both. A hybrid product will be less expensive than purchasing life insurance and long-term-care insurance separately (but it will often be more expensive than purchasing a standalone long-term-care insurance policy).

The products vary in the details, but the general idea is that they allow you to purchase a cash-value life insurance policy and use a portion of that policy for long-term care benefits, if necessary, while keeping the rest as a death benefit that will be paid to your beneficiary. If long-term-care benefits are used, the death benefit may be reduced.

These hybrids usually allow a buyer to purchase a fixed deferred annuity with a long-term-care rider attached. The annuity may pay out for a specific number of years or for life. For example, say you deposited $150,000 into an annuity. The annuity would pay you long-term-care benefits of approximately $4,700 a month for thirty-six months. For an additional cost, you could get the $4,700 monthly benefit for life.

There are a few important differences between traditional policies and hybrid versions:

- *Cost and payment structure:* Hybrid policies are, typically, funded in one lump sum—or in payments over only a certain number of years—which have to total at least $50,000. This could mean you'd have a hard time coming up with the cost. On the other hand, this structure protects you from the premium hikes that are standard in traditional long-term-care policies.

- *Benefits:* Hybrid policies usually have lower benefit levels per dollar than traditional long-term-care policies. They also may not offer other features, such as inflation protection, which could be available with traditional policies. With medical costs rising, this could be a serious concern. You might, for example, buy a policy that would give you benefits that are large enough to cover three years of long-term care today, but when the time comes for you to actually make a claim, you may find out that that amount only covers two years of care.

- *Partnerships:* If you're a middle-income American, you may qualify for the Long-Term Care Partnership Program, a joint federal-state program that allows long-term-care insurance buyers to get financial help through Medicaid if they've exhausted their long-term-care assurance, while still protecting some of their assets. Hybrid policies are not eligible for this program.

In order to decide whether a hybrid or traditional policy would be best for your circumstances, ask yourself, "How much life insurance do I really need?" If your home is paid off, your children are self-supporting, and leaving them a financial legacy isn't one of your priorities, you probably don't need life insurance. In that case, you'd be better off buying a long-term-care insurance policy. Even if you do decide you need both long-term-care insurance and life insurance, the up-front payment for a hybrid policy may not be the best use of your money.

You also have other choices besides stand-alone traditional policies and hybrid policies. Many life insurance policies offer accelerated-benefit riders, which allow you to draw on your death benefit ahead of time to fund long-term care and other costs. (There are eligibility requirements, such as a long-term need for services.) Permanent life insurance policies also allow loans and withdrawals from cash value if you have enough. You could use this money toward long-term-care costs, although your death benefit will be reduced if the loans are not repaid.

As with every other retirement strategy that we've discussed, we recommend that you not try to sort out these options by yourself. Get advice from your trusted advisor—*not* a sales agent, who will make a commission off selling policies—but avoid what would be the worst option of all: not doing anything at all. Planning for long-term care is an essential part of a wise retirement strategy.

The basic purpose of any type of insurance is to buy peace of mind. Annuities can put your mind to rest when it comes to your own retirement needs, and life insurance might free you from your worries about your family after your death. A long-term-care insurance policy can give you yet another level of peace of mind.

COMBINING LONG-TERM-CARE INSURANCE WITH HYBRID-INDEXED ANNUITIES

With some hybrid-indexed annuities, you can choose to add an income rider that will provide a guaranteed income for life when the owner decides to start the income somewhere down the road. In addition, the income rider carries a health-care provision that if the owner cannot perform two out of six activities of daily living, then his family doctor would send a letter to the insurance company, and the income payments would be doubled for up to five years for either spouse. These income payments can be started and stopped as needed, and after the fifth year, reverted to the original income. The checks are made out directly to the annuity owner and can be used for whatever medical costs are incurred. The cost for the income rider is one percent or less annually.

WHAT ELSE CAN YOU DO?

Even if retirement is just around the corner, there are other steps you can do now that will help you get ready.

- *Create a plan to ensure you won't have a lapse in medical coverage after you retire:* Unexpected and uninsured medical expenses could seriously diminish any retirement funds you have. Make sure there's no gap between when your medical coverage expires and the date when you'll become eligible for Medicare.

- *Update your estate-planning documents:* Estate preparation and protecting your loved ones from the unexpected is another area that needs close attention when you're nearing retirement.

- *Make sure you have a will and that you have an assigned power of attorney:* If you've never created these documents or if your circumstances have changed since they were created (for example, your children are grown now or you have accumulated more assets), meet with an attorney to ensure your heirs will receive your legacy exactly as you wish and in the most tax-efficient manner possible. You should also create a living will to ensure that your medical care is carried out in the way you want.

- *Discuss your life insurance portfolio with your advisor:* If you bought life insurance years ago, you probably had other goals in mind than you do now. When your family is young, life insurance is intended to replace your income in the event you die prematurely. You might have wanted life insurance to pay off your mortgage or pay for your children's education. At this point in your life, your house may be paid for and your children out on their own. A life insurance policy now would need to serve other purposes. Have an experienced and trusted advisor look over your coverage to make sure it is still suitable for your current situation.

- *Stop paying for your grown children:* You paid all the expenses of raising your children, but once they're adults, they're no longer your responsibility. Put your retirement needs first. Get your own financial house on a solid foundation before you try to help your kids.

- *If you have a term life insurance policy that is convertible, sell it instead of letting it expire:* There are companies that will pay the premiums and give you a lump sum (depending on your life expectancy) that could be $35,000 or $40,000 on a $500,000 policy.

- *Pay off high-interest credit cards:* Say you have $10,000 in a savings account where it's collecting very little interest. It makes more sense to use it to pay off a credit card balance that's charging 18 percent interest.

- *If you're behind in saving for your retirement, don't be lured into taking investment risks:* Remember Las Vegas is not a good place for funding your retirement—and neither is Wall Street.

- *Don't borrow money from whatever retirement savings you have:* Instead, make a practice of keeping an emergency fund on hand so you won't be tempted to dip into your retirement funds in a crisis. A good emergency fund should have at least six months of income set aside in a separate account.

- *Control your "urge to splurge":* Any retirement strategy involves a trade-off between your current consumption and consumption later in retirement. Don't think of it as denying yourself. Instead, remind yourself that the money you save now will allow you to enjoy your life more later.

- *Live with urgency:* You don't need to fear the future, but you should appreciate the present moment and the opportunities it offers. Seize each and every day to stay healthy and happy. You can apply this to all aspects of life, from what you do during retirement to the way you save money throughout your working life. A sense of urgency is a call to action. It can motivate you to prepare for a great retirement.

- *Make the decision to retire based on your financial assets, not your age:* While you might have a certain age in mind, it can be more worthwhile to create a financial strategy that helps enable you to retire based on your finances instead of your age. This helps ensure that you have enough money for the rest of your life.

- *Start today:* The longer you wait, the harder it will be to create the retirement you want to live.

BE FLEXIBLE

Retirement planning isn't something you do once and then you're done. And it's not something that has to be done completely before you retire. Instead, it's an ongoing process. Diane Savage, a Certified Financial Planner™ and educator, says, "Retirement-income planning is not static and is not a one-time decision. It requires attention throughout retirement with many course adjustments."[61]

She goes on to say, "So many of the factors related to retirement-income management are not controllable even though we like to think they are." As human beings, we'd like to think we're in control of what the future holds, but of course, we never are. The best you can do is plan wisely as soon as possible and then make adjustments, as needed, as you go along.

---

61 Robert Powell, "Five Strategies to Get the Most Social Security," MarketWatch, March 29, 2014, www.marketwatch.com/story/five-strategies-to-get-the-most-social-security-2014-03-15.

But whatever you do, don't do nothing at all! No matter how old you are when you begin, talk to your financial advisor now and begin working on smart retirement strategies.

FACT

There are steps you can take today to ensure you have a secure retirement!

CHAPTER 10

FACT OR FICTION:
FAR FROM BEING THE GOLDEN YEARS,
RETIREMENT IS A TIME OF POOR HEALTH
AND FEWER OPPORTUNITIES TO ENJOY LIFE

A t the beginning of each of the chapters in this book, we used a different story to introduce our topic. We used these stories as metaphors to shape your understanding of what we wanted to tell you. Psychologists tell us that all human beings rely on metaphors to understand the world around them, and the kind of metaphors they use will mold their perception of reality.

Suppose, for example, you walk into a new job, and one of your fellow employees says to you, "Welcome to the monkey house!" Throughout the day, you hear your new colleagues continually use metaphorical language such as "loony bin," "nuthouse," and "funny farm." You go home at the end of the day seriously concerned about your decision to take this job. In the days that follow, you look for—and find—evidence that indicates that your colleagues are right: your new job's expectations are irrational and insane.

Now imagine, instead, that when you walked into your new office building, someone said to you, "Welcome to our wonderful playhouse!" This time, throughout the day you heard words such as "think tank," "creative exploration," "discovery channel," and "collaborative sandbox." At the end of day, you'll probably go home happily anticipating your new career. Instead of expecting insanity, you're looking forward to opportunities for creativity and innovation.

How you think about retirement will also be shaped by the metaphors you use, which will, in turn, shape your actual retirement experience. A study carried out at the University of Montana found that retirees and soon-to-be-retired people use a variety of metaphors for retirement.[62] These included language that implied a wide range of possible retirement outcomes:

- "loss of identity"
- "new freedom"
- "nothing to do but wait to die"
- "a milestone"
- "put out to the pasture"
- "a new life"
- "no longer in the limelight"
- "putting down a heavy load"

62 Steven R. Phillips and Betsy Wackernagle Bach, "The Metaphors of Retirement: Cutting Cords, Disentangling from Webs, and Heading for Pasture," University of Montana Scholar Works, scholarworks.umt.edu/cgi/viewcontent.cgi?article=1006&context=comm unications_pubs.

As you can see, retirement metaphors can be either positive or negative. The ones you choose to use will shape not only how you perceive retirement before you retire but also how you experience it after you retire.

When you think about retirement, chances are you feel a range of emotions that include both anticipation and fear. That's only natural. Think about how you felt before all the big milestones of your life. You probably entered into marriage with both joy and nervousness. You anticipated your first child with a mixture of happiness and worry. If you made a major move across the country to take a new job, you likely felt a combination of excitement and dread. The reality of each also included elements of both joy and stress; it takes time to adjust to even a good change in your life.

So it makes sense that when you think about retirement, you feel a similar combination of emotions.

As you consider retirement, you'll be asking yourself things such as:

- "How will I occupy my days?"

- "Will my spouse and I get on each other's nerves?"

- "Will I have enough income?"

- "Will I have more time for the things I love—or will I be bored?"

Most of us can't use our parents' experience as our model for retirement. Our generation is venturing into new territory. Our parents' and grandparents' retirement plans came from a long tradition with its roots in the past. Twenty-first-century retirement is different from what it was even a generation ago.

TWENTY-FIRST-CENTURY RETIREMENT

Back in ancient China, employers (warlords and land barons) were generally more knowledgeable than their employees (serfs) in business and financial matters. These employers believed it was their responsibility to provide financial rewards to long-term loyal employees during their income-producing years as well as during their non-income-producing retirement years. This was the birth of defined benefits, also known as guaranteed lifetime income annuities.

However, the employer's traditional sense of responsibility to provide defined benefits began to change in the late 1980s. In 1985, if an employer promised $1,000 a month at retirement through a defined-benefit plan, workers could rest assured they would receive $1,000 per month for the rest of their lives. As in ancient China, the employer took on the interest rate, life expectancy, and market-risk costs associated with accumulating sufficient assets to pay the promised income for life. However, toward the end of the 1980s, the economic realities of declining interest rates from previous double-digit highs, increasing life expectancy, and greater market volatility (the October 1987 market implosion, for example) caused employers to become concerned about controlling the increasing expenses involved with funding defined-benefit plans.

During the late 1980s, many options were reviewed to help the employer manage the promised retirement-income cost liability, which was being hammered by lower interest rates, increasing longevity, and market volatility. The most touted answer among several options led to the rise of the 401(k) plan. The 401(k) almost, but not completely, eliminated employer fiduciary and cost liability by shifting the burden to the plan participant. Meanwhile, plan participants are doing a less than acceptable job of funding their retirement-income needs, according to the President's Council of Economic Advisers 2012 report, *Supporting Retirement for American Families*.[63]

Neither employers nor lawmakers nor stockbrokers nor plan participants will claim they were the primary cause of the shift from defined benefit plans to 401(k) plans. However, with the possible exception of stockbrokers, who continue to make money, and employers, who believe they have eliminated most of their fiduciary liability, all of them now believe we need to return to defined benefits (a lifetime-income annuity). But how?

Currently, two available options allow 401(k) plan participants to convert a major part of their 401(k) account to defined-benefit (lifetime-income annuity) savings in their account. The US Treasury Department has developed a deferred-income annuity (DIA) for 401(k) plans. This annuity addresses the issue of living too long, but it lacks flexibility in several areas. Also available is a specially designed FIA with a living-income benefit rider. Once the FIA is added to the 401(k) plan, participants have the option to move a portion of their savings account balance to this annuity. The FIA is designed to provide more flexibility than the US Treasury Department DIA. It can stand alone, or it can complement the longevity annuity if both options are selected by the plan participant.

Twenty-first-century retirement has changed in many ways. A mandatory retirement age made sense in an age when most workers did physical labor, since a worker's value was proportional to physical strength, which inevitably declined with age. In today's economy, however, a worker's value is related more to intellectual ability than physical strength. Consequently, many people are choosing to retire

---

63 "Supporting Retirement for American Families," Executive Office of the President's Council of Economic Advisers, February 2, 2012, www.whitehouse.gov/sites/default/files/cea_retirement_report_01312012_final.pdf.

later in life. After all, if American presidents in their sixties can run the country and lead the world, why should we have to retire from our jobs at the same age?

In today's retirement world, far fewer people go straight from full-time work to not working at all. Now we're more likely to work part time after retirement. We might turn a hobby we've always loved into a business or even pursue a second career. This is partly for financial reasons (because we need to find a way to stretch our retirement income), but it's also because we're staying healthy longer than previous generations did, which means we may have the opportunity to explore new interests after we retire from our first career. Because we live longer and healthier lives, we may also decide to delay retirement until we're in our seventies.

When you're going to work every day, working forty-hour (or more) work weeks, a life of leisure can sometimes seem very attractive. You may forget that your work also helps give meaning to your life. Feeling as though you're useful, that you're contributing something to the world, gives you self-respect and a sense of identity that constant downtime never can.

Retirees keep busy in all sorts of ways. One man continued to work on his farm after he retired from his other works. He was driving a tractor and milking cows well into his eighties. A retired schoolteacher fulfilled a lifetime dream by becoming ordained as a minister, which allowed her to pastor a small rural church. A former factory worker now drives a school bus five days a week, tends a bar one night a week, and does some woodworking in his free time. A jewelry maker returned to work when she was seventy, crafting jewelry that she now sells at craft fairs and art festivals.

According to the Transamerica Center for Retirement Studies, not all retirees go back to work because they need the money. Forty percent of the retirees surveyed did so because they enjoy their work.[64] You may be ready to ease up on some of your work responsibilities while preserving the things you like best about it. Working part time after retirement can give you the best of both worlds. For example, you could have greater flexibility to choose when you work and when you don't. You might be able to work more from home.

Easing into retirement gradually can be good for you, physically and emotionally. It can even be good for your marriage. Adjusting to retirement is a big transition, one that can be handled creatively and positively—or negatively. Experts have found that people who retire "cold turkey," often experience depression, an increase in stress-related diseases, weight gain, and marital conflict.[65]

A 2013 study by the Institute of Foreign Affairs, a London-based think tank, surveyed nearly nine thousand people between the ages of fifty and seventy. The people surveyed were interviewed twice, with the second interview two to three years after the first. The study looked at the changes in health between the two interviews and found that people who were retired at the time of their first interview were 41 percent more likely to later suffer from clinical depression. They were also 63 percent more likely to develop a physical condition. People who were still in the workforce, on the other hand, were far more likely to report their health was "very good" or "excellent." [66]

Part-time work can provide the exercise people need to stay healthy. Research has shown that even young people lose physical strength quickly when they're inactive, and even older people can regain strength when they exercise regularly. Being engaged in some

64 "15th Annual Transamerica Retirement Survey," Transamerica Center for Retirement Studies, https://www.transamericacenter.org/retirement-research/15th-annual-retirement-survey.
65 Kelsey Sheehy, "Want a Healthy, Rich Retirement? Keep Working," USA Today, June 6, 2015, http://www.usatoday.com/story/money/personalfinance/2015/06/06/nerdwallet-working-in-retirement/28435685.
66 Ibid.

form of work also exercises your brain. This isn't just a figure of speech. The more it's used, the better your brain works, as is the case with other parts of your body. A 2014 report by Merrill Lynch backed this up, finding that more than 65 percent of retirees say that not working speeds the decline of their mental abilities.[67]

If you're considering part-time work after retirement, think about what you like best about working. Does helping others give meaning to your life? Do you enjoy socializing with coworkers? Is creativity an essential part of what you want your life to be? Also consider what you *don't* like about work. Long workdays, paperwork, tedious tasks, and rush-hour commutes might be things you want to avoid now that you have a choice. Take time to determine what will make you happiest.

There are several options for you to consider. As an experienced employee, you may have a lot to offer your current employer, even after retirement. Your employer might be willing to allow you to work part time or let you move into a role that's less demanding or requires fewer hours. If you're a teacher, you might want to work as a substitute teacher or even fill in long term for someone on maternity leave. Some people continue to work in their fields as contractors and consultants, which gives them the freedom to pick and choose how much they want to work. Another option is to share with others the professional wisdom and insight you've accumulated over the years of your career. You could teach, mentor, or become a public speaker.

You may also want to use your retirement to try out completely different roles and responsibilities. While you probably won't have time or energy to go to medical school and become a neurosurgeon, there are many other roles and skills with which you could experiment. Frank McCourt, author of the Pulitzer Prize–winning *Angela's*

---

67 "Work in Retirement: Myths and Motivations," Merrill Lynch, mlaem.fs.ml.com/content/dam/ML/Articles/pdf/MLWM_Work-in-Retirement_2014.pdf.

Ashes, didn't start writing until he was in his sixties, after a thirty-year career as an English teacher. Who knows what *you* might accomplish when you have more time in your life?

Surveys reveal that almost 60 percent of new retirees seek part-time work within a year. The need for additional income is one reason why retirees are going back to work, but the survey's participants listed social, intellectual, and achievement factors as often as they did financial.[68]

But that doesn't mean the way we think about retirement doesn't have important financial implications. Most of us want to do more than our parents did during retirement. At the same time, we have to find different ways to fund our retirement. Our parents' retirement plans probably looked something like this: they would live off their Social Security income, pension income, and interest on their savings (while never touching their principal). This plan probably won't work for most of today's retirees.

It's not easy to know how much money you're actually going to need during retirement, so it's hard to know exactly how much to save. No matter how many factors you take into consideration, there will always be two that you can't predict exactly: how long you (and your spouse) will live and the rate of inflation during your retirement.

Many financial advisors add a third unknown to that list: your portfolio's rate of return during your retirement. As a result, people who have bought into the American love affair with risk end up hoping that their portfolio's rate of return will be what bails out their retirement. But the primary factor that will determine if you'll have financial independence in retirement is not what the stock market does; it's how much you save and invest during your working years.

---

68 Sienna Kossman, "8 Great Part-Time Jobs for Retirees," *US News & World Report,* June 12, 2013, http://money.usnews.com/money/retirement/slideshows/8-great-part-time-jobs-for-retirees.

Thanks to FIAs, we don't have to include your investments' rate of return in our list of unknowns.

A good financial advisor can help you make conservative assumptions about the unknowns that will affect your retirement. It's safe to say, for example, that a healthy sixty-five-year-old couple should plan on financing a thirty-year retirement, while assuming that inflation will continue to increase at the 3 percent rate it has historically.

Given those numbers, retirement will be the most expensive purchase you're ever going to make.

Think about it. The average cost of a house is about $190,000, while your retirement could easily cost more than $1 million. Even allowing for Social Security and any pension funds, retirement is still more expensive than anything else you'll ever buy (even more expensive than your children's college education). When you look at it that way, don't you think it's important you get your money's worth?

We'd like you to start thinking about retirement as a time in your life that will begin when you achieve financial independence. When that's the case, the first decade or two of retirement can also be a time that will provide you with new opportunities for finding meaning in life, a time when you can enjoy experiences you had no time for while you were working. The later decades of your retirement may have different income needs, so it might be useful to think of retirement as having two phases. Using this two-phase definition as the foundation for your financial plan will give you a new perspective on the retirement income you'll need. It will make that most expensive purchase of your life also the most worthwhile purchase of your life.

THE COST OF RETIREMENT

The cost of retirement has two elements that need to be considered. The first answers the question "What do I do with today's assets to fund my retirement?" The second and equally important element answers the question "How much am I going to spend each year for the thirty to forty years of my retirement?" A lot of financial planners build a portfolio that is focused only on accumulation, independent of your retirement liability.

To estimate your retirement liability, you need to determine what your current income's replacement rate will be. In other words, what will change when you retire? If you're making $75,000 today and then you retire tomorrow, what things will need to be replaced from an income perspective in order to maintain the lifestyle you want during the first decade or two of your retirement?

"Consumption smoothing"—also called the "life-cycle model"—is a way to think about the transition into retirement. You don't want to have a sudden radical change in your lifestyle, not if you can prevent that by planning ahead with the right retirement strategies. Using FIAs will allow you to create an income stream you can count on.

Keep in mind that your expenses will be different during retirement in a few ways that will be to your benefit.

- You'll no longer have to be saving for retirement.

- Your tax situation will be different; not all of your income will be taxable.

- You'll no longer have work-related expenses. (For example, because you have more time, you may eat at home more often than you eat out. Without a work commute, you will probably spend less on gasoline and car maintenance or train and bus fares.)

Typically, retirement planners inflate first-year retirement expenses by 3 percent to determine what their clients will need throughout the rest of their retirement. We'd like to suggest that a better model uses the two-phase notion of retirement. Odds are good that you'll want to spend more money in your sixties and seventies than you will in your eighties and nineties.

Recently, researchers have been studying what's called the "retirement consumption puzzle." They've found that consumption changes during retirement. During the earlier phase of retirement, people's consumption may not be all that different from what it was before they retired. If anything, it may be a bit higher than it was before. As people move into retirement's second phase, however, they often become less mobile, which generally means they spend less. This decreased consumption level is maintained until late in the second phase, when health-care expenses usually go up. According to statistics from the US Census Bureau, the average sixty-five-year-old spends about 10 percent of total consumption on health care. (That percentage is constant regardless of whether the individual is high income, middle income, or low income.) By the time that same individual is eighty-five, about 20 percent of total consumption will be going to health care.[69]

However, a recent Morningstar report found that this increase in health-care spending is offset by a decline in spending in other areas such as travel and leisure activities.[70] On average, real (inflation-adjusted) spending declines approximately 1 percent annually

---

69 US Census Bureau, http://www.census.gov.
70 David Blanchett, "Estimating the True Cost of Retirement," corporate.morningstar.com/ib/documents/MethodologyDocuments/ResearchPapers/Blanchett_True-Cost-of-Retirement.pdf.

throughout both phases of retirement. The report concludes that typical expense models for retirement planning may be overestimating the cost of retirement by as much as 20 percent. Obviously, these results will vary, depending on your unique circumstances. Still, the report indicates that, early in their retirement, most retirees can spend a bit more than was previously believed on activities they might not be able to enjoy later in life.

The other factor you'll need to consider is what's known as "longevity risk." Living longer is a good thing, but it's also the greatest of all retirement risks. Funding a retirement for twenty years costs a lot more than funding it for fifteen years. In the past, one of the key means that individuals used to fund their retirements were through defined-benefit plans. These plans worked much like insurance does since the risk of living too long was pooled. For every person who lived to be ninety-five or one hundred, someone else would die at age sixty-five or seventy. Now, though, we have defined-contribution plans, and risk is no longer pooled. This means that most us should plan to live to be ninety-five or one hundred, just to be safe.

If you want to figure out what that means in terms of your retirement plan, there's a simple math formula that might help you out.

THE RULE OF 72

The Rule of 72 is a way to figure out approximately how long it will take for your money to double at a given annual compound interest rate, or rate of return. It's pretty simple: you divide seventy-two by the annual growth rate or interest rate.

Let's say you have retirement savings that are returning at 6 percent a year:

$$72 \div 6 = 12$$

It would take about twelve years for your investment to double.

This equation will also help you if you're trying to figure out what annual growth, or interest, rate you need to double your money in X number of years. Say, for example, you want to double your money in ten years:

$$72 \div X = 10$$

If you remember grade-school arithmetic, the answer to this equation can be found by turning it around:

$$72 \div 10 = X$$

In other words, you'd need a 7.2 percent interest rate to achieve your goal.

The Rule of 72 works pretty well for growth rates between 6 and 10 percent. Beyond this range, it's less accurate, but it's still a good way to help you understand what you need as you make decisions about your retirement strategies, such as how much to save and when to retire. If you need to step up your savings plan to meet your goals, you'll be able to see that. And when you see just how much your savings can accumulate through compounding, that can be a real incentive to save!

BOTTOM LINE

An FIA will give you a guaranteed income for the length of your retirement, no matter how long you live, but you still need to determine how much that income should be. You can't predict the future, but you *can* create a realistic retirement budget that takes into account the changing expenses of both phases of your retirement.

You need to think consciously and intentionally about how you choose to define your retirement. The metaphors you use to describe this phase of your life will shape your behaviors now. Your retirement could be "the end of the road," but wouldn't you rather your retirement be "a new beginning"? If you think of your retirement in terms of "a new door that opens when old doors close" or "a new adventure," you can choose the financial strategies you'll need. A good retirement advisor will help you consider all the complex factors we've discussed in order to get you where you want to be in the years ahead.

The fact is you're not at the end of the road. You're at a crossroads. The retirement strategy you make now will decide the road you take.

FACT
With the right financial strategies, your retirement can be one of the most meaningful times in your life.

CONCLUSION

We hope we've helped you sort the facts out from the fictions. Remember, these are the facts:

- You need a trusted advisor to help you plan for your retirement.

- Your current financial advisor may not be giving you the advice you need to plan for your retirement.

- A pension fund no longer guarantees a secure retirement.

- The brokerage industry is ethically and functionally flawed.

- Many private-equity firms have hidden costs that are robbing your investment.

- Your actual stock-market returns will probably be far less than you'd expected.

- You shouldn't be gambling with your hard-earned retirement money.

- With FIAs, you never lose your money.

- There are steps you can take today to ensure you have a secure retirement!

- With the right financial strategies, your retirement can be one of the most meaningful times in your life.

THE ULTIMATE RETIREMENT STRATEGY

Every day, an increasing number of retirees who are concerned about their income begin to purchase annuities. This gives them an additional paycheck every single month during their retirement. Many uneducated or untrained people like to tear down the annuity concept. It may be that they simply don't get it. Or they may be thinking about annuity products that were around years back when the insurance company kept your money if you didn't collect it all in payouts. Annuities have changed a lot since then.

Even so, they are not designed to be the ultimate solution for your retirement-income needs. But they might play an important role in your overall retirement-income strategy. You see, keeping all your assets in one place over the long run is probably never a great idea. But what if you could spread out and protect some of your assets by purchasing an annuity, guaranteeing income that you can't outlive?

We're not saying you should take all your assets and purchase an annuity contract. But you might want to take just a portion of your retirement nest egg and purchase an annuity. Withdrawals or payouts from the annuity can help provide you with enough income to cover your basic living expenses, giving you greater financial confidence in retirement. Wouldn't that help take some pressure off of your retirement-income planning? Think about it.

Annuities are really good at guaranteeing you an income for life. Here at Secure Retirement Strategies, we have proprietary annuity income strategies that could give you significantly more guaranteed income during retirement—income you can't outlive. And the icing on the cake is there's no risk of losing your principal to stock-market volatility. Imagine never losing a penny of your total account value—

principal and gains—when the market has *any* downward correction and making a great return when the market goes up!

Annuities are designed this way for a reason. They're a tool to help round out your retirement-income strategy, and a tool that may work well in your situation. The way they're structured is exactly what makes them work and what makes them effective.

You don't have to take our word for it. Do your research. Check out a study done on FIAs by the Wharton School. Find out why celebrities such as Shaquille O'Neil and Magic Johnson depend on FIAs to maintain the lifestyle to which they've become accustomed. (In fact, FIAs are so safe that O. J. Simpson was able to retain his income, despite his many legal troubles.) Index annuities could be the ultimate retirement strategy you need.

We'd love to tell you more. At Secure Retirement Strategies, we're here to help.

REFERENCES

Arends, Brett. "Why Are Stock Prices So High? Follow the Borrowed Money." MarketWatch. May 7, 2015. www.marketwatch.com/story/why-are-stock-prices-so-high-follow-the-borrowed-money-2015-05-07.

"AXA Equitable to Pay New York DFS $20M Fine Over Annuity Changes." *Insurance Journal.* March 18, 2014.

Babbel, David F. "Wharton Financial Institutions Center Policy Brief: Personal Finance." Wharton. 2015.

William Baldwin. "State Pension Funds: As Broke as Ever." Forbes. January 15, 2016. http://www.forbes.com/sites/baldwin/2016/01/16/state-pension-funds-as-broke-as-ever/#5a216ac54900.

Bankrate. http://www.bankrate.com/cd.aspx.

Blanchett, David. "Estimating the True Cost of Retirement." corporate.morningstar.com/ib/documents/MethodologyDocuments/ResearchPapers/Blanchett_True-Cost-of-Retirement.pdf.

Bogle, John. "Building a Fiduciary Society." Bogle Financial Markets Research Center. March 13, 2009. www.vanguard.com/bogle_site/sp20090313.html.

Bowley, Graham. "In Striking Shift, Small Investors Flee Stock Market." *New York Times.* August 21, 2010. www.nytimes.com/2010/08/22/business/22invest.html.

Brooks, Rodney. "Managing Your Retirement Nest Egg and Making It Last as Long as You Do." *Washington Post.* February 27, 2016.

Brooks, Rodney. "Tips for People Behind in Retirement Savings." *USA Today.* March 24, 2015.

Brubaker, Harold. "Continuing-Care Retirement Community Choice Requires Diligence." Philly. May 11, 2015. articles.philly.com/2015-05-11/business/62005316_1_continuing-care-retirement-community-ccrcs-pennsylvania-insurance-department.

Bureau of Economic Analysis. "Measuring the Nation's Economy." https://www.bea.gov.

"Calculators: Life Expectancy." Social Security Adminstration. https://www.ssa.gov/planners/lifeexpectancy.html.

CEM Benchmarking. "The Time Has Come for Standardized Total Cost Disclosure for Private Equity." April 2015. http://www.cembenchmarking.com/Files/Documents/CEM_article_-_The_time_has_come_for_standardized_total_cost_disclosure_for_private_equity.pdf.

Center for Retirement Research at Boston College. "Annuities: Useful but Little Understood." Squared Away Blog. May 28, 2015. squaredawayblog.bc.edu/squared-away/annuities-useful-but-little-understood.

Clements, Jonathan. "7 Lies Investors Tell Themselves." MarketWatch. May 26, 2015. www.marketwatch.com/story/7-lies-investors-tell-themselves-2015-05-25.

CNBC.com. "One-Third of Americans Have No Financial Plan, Study Says." NBC News. April 29, 2015. www.nbcnews.com/business/personal-finance/one-third-americans-have-no-financial-plan-study-says-n350351.

Cohen, Aubry. "Retirement: How Not to Go Broke Before You Die." *USA Today.* May 18, 2015.

Condon, Bernard. "AP Analysis: More 'Phony Numbers' in Reports as Stocks Rise." Associated Press. June 8, 2015. news.yahoo.com/experts-worry-phony-numbers-misleading-investors-070228914.html.

"Day Trading El Dorado." *Forbes.* June 12, 2000.

Dowd, Casey. "5 Things to Do Now if You're Near Retirement."
Fox Business. May 22, 2015. http://www.foxbusiness.com/
features/2015/05/21/5-things-to-do-now-if-youre-near-retirement.html.

Driebusch, Corrie. "Stocks Tumble as Investors Flee to Safety." *Wall Street Journal.* February 11, 2016.

Epperson, Sharon. "Worried About Outliving Your Money? Consider This." CNBC. May 21, 2015. www.cnbc.com/2015/05/21/worried-about-outliving-your-money-consider-annuities.html.

Farrell, Paul B. "'Bull's-Eye Investors' Still Lose."
MarketWatch. August 17, 2004. www.marketwatch.com/story/
hitting-the-bulls-eye-and-losing-all-the-same.

Farrell, Paul B. "It's a Game of Musical Chairs at the Wall Street Casino—And the Loser Is You." MarketWatch. April 3, 2015, www.marketwatch.com/story/its-a-game-of-musical-chairs-at-the-wall-street-casino-and-the-loser-is-you-2015-04-03.

Farrell, Paul B. "The More You Trade the Less You Earn."
MarketWatch. August 6, 2001. http://www.marketwatch.com/story/
the-more-you-trade-the-less-you-earn.

Faunce, Justin. "3 Ways to Boost the Odds Your Savings
Will Last a Lifetime." June 4, 2015. www.linkedin.com/
pulse/3-ways-boost-odds-your-savings-last-lifetime-justin-faunce.

"Fiduciary Rule Divides Fixed And Variable Annuity Worlds." Annuity News. July 30, 2015. annuitynews.com/Article/Fiduciary-Rule-Divides-Fixed-And-Variable-Annuity-Worlds/668435#.Vt2qmsfyeFI.

"15th Annual Transamerica Retirement Survey." Transamerica
Center for Retirement Studies. https://www.transamericacenter.org/
retirement-research/15th-annual-retirement-survey.

"Financial Engines & Aon Hewitt find 401(k) Participants Who Use Professional Help Are Better Off Than Those Who Do Not." financial engines. May 13, 2014. http://ir.financialengines.com/phoenix.zhtml?c=233599&p=irol-newsArticle&ID=1930183.

Ford, Mark Morgan. "What You Should Ask Your Money Manager Today—Right Now." Early to Rise. March 7, 2016. www.earlytorise.com/what-you-should-ask-your-money-manager-today-right-now.

Fuscaldo, Donna. "Here's What You Need to Know About Annuities." *Fox Business.* December 30, 2013. www.foxbusiness.com/features/2013/12/30/heres-what-need-to-know-about-annuities.html.

Hackenthal, Andreas, Michael Halliassos, and Tullio Jappelli. "Financial Advisors: A Case of Babysitters?" Social Science Research Network (SSRN). ssrn.com/abstract=1360440 or http://dx.doi.org/10.2139/ssrn.1360440.

Haithcock, Stan. "My RA Should Be My Annuity." MarketWatch. March 4, 2014.

Haugk, Kristin. "Wall Street Regulations: When the Wolf is Guarding the Henhouse." Wealthy Retirement. November 12, 2015. http://wealthyretirement.com/wolf-is-guarding-the-henhouse-finra-regulatory-notice-15-37.

Hebeler, Henry K. "Retiring? Why You Might Need More Money Than You Think." MarketWatch. April 22, 2015. www.marketwatch.com/story/retiring-why-you-might-need-more-money-than-you-think-2015-04-22.

Hellmich, Nanci. "One-Third of all US Workers Have Almost No Retirement Savings." *USA Today.* April 21, 2015.

Hill, Catey. "Got an IRA? Chances Are It's Too Risky." MarketWatch. October 30, 2014.

Holland, Kelley. "How to Navigate the Retirement Danger Zone." CNBC. May 26, 2015. www.cnbc.com/2015/05/26/gate-the-retirement-danger-zone.html.

Hulbert, Mark. "Simple Math Does Not Support the Bulls." MarketWatch. October 23, 2013. www.marketwatch.com/story/simple-math-does-not-support-the-bulls-2013-10-23.

Jaffe, Chuck. "Why the Big Broker Behind Your Financial Advisor Might Be Working Against You." MarketWatch. April 4, 2015.

Kahneman, Daniel. *Thinking Fast and Slow* New York: Farrar, Straus and Giroux, 2011.

Kane, Libby. "9 Tricks Casinos Use to Make You Spend More Money." *Business Insider*. August 19, 2014. http://www.businessinsider.com/how-casinos-make-you-spend-money-2014-8.

Kaplan, Eve. "Annuities: The Good, the Bad and the Ugly," *Forbes*, July 15, 2015.

Kelland, Kate. "John Coates, Former Wall Street Trader, Studies Neuroscience Behind Financial Risk Taking." *Huffington Post*. December 10, 2012. www.huffingtonpost.com/2012/10/10/john-coates-wall-street-trader-neuroscientist_n_1953661.html.

Klein, Robert. "Fixed-Index Annuities as Bond Alternatives?" MarketWatch. August 21, 2013. www.marketwatch.com/story/fixed-index-annuities-as-bonds-alternative-2013-08-21.

Köppenheffer, Matt. "The Cold, Hard Truth About Brokers and Financial Advisors." The Motley Fool. March 20, 2012. http://www.fool.com/investing/general/2012/03/20/the-cold-hard-truth-about-brokers-and-financial-a.aspx.

Kossman, Sienna. "8 Great Part-Time Jobs for Retirees." *US News & World Report*. June 12, 2013. http://money.usnews.com/money/retirement/slideshows/8-great-part-time-jobs-for-retirees.

Lankford, Kimberly. "Protection for Fixed Annuities." *Kiplinger's Personal Finance*. February 2016.

Leising, Matthew. "NYSE's Next Owner Says Small U.S. Investors Get Ripped Off." *Bloomberg Business*. November 5, 2013. www.bloomberg.com/news/articles/2013-11-05/ice-has-informed-view-of-how-to-integrate-nyse-ceo-says.

Phalippou, Ludovic. "Beware of Venturing into Private Equity." The Journal of Economic Perspectives. Vol. 23, No. 1 (Winter, 2009), 147–166.

Mahmudova, Anora. "Stocks Are Overpriced, Overleveraged, Headed for Trouble." MarketWatch. March 25, 2015. www.marketwatch.com/story/stocks-are-overpriced-overleveraged-headed-for-trouble-2015-03-25.

"Market Gains Drive Retirement Balances Higher But Too Much Stock Could Put Savings at Risk. Fidelity Analysis Finds." Fidelity. www.fidelity.com/about-fidelity/employer-services/market-gains-drive-retirement-balances-higher.

McNair, Andrew. "RIP Traditional Long-Term-Care Insurance." MarketWatch. April 10, 2015. www.marketwatch.com/story/rip-traditional-long-term-care-insurance-2015-04-10.

"Work in Retirement: Myths and Motivations." Merrill Lynch. mlaem.fs.ml.com/content/dam/ML/Articles/pdf/MLWM_Work-in-Retirement_2014.pdf.

"Millenials and Money: Part Young Idealists, Part Old Souls." Northwestern Mutual. April 7, 2015. https://www.northwesternmutual.com/news-room/122886.

Mims, Rod. "Fixed Indexed Annuities: Accumulation First." Broker World. February 2016.

Moberg, David. "Central States Pension Fund Prepares to Spash Hundreds of Thousands of Workers' Pensions." October 5, 2015. http://inthesetimes.com/working/entry/18472/central_states_pension_fund_prepares_to_slash_hundreds_of_thousands_of_work.

Moisand, Dan. "What Older Workers Can and Can't Do with Their 401(k) Plans." MarketWatch. October 24, 2014.

Morningstar. "CGM Focus Fund." http://performance.morningstar.com/fund/performance-return.action?t=CGMFX.

Morgenson, Gretchen. "Pension Funds Can Only Guess at Private Equity's Cost." *New York Times*. May 1, 2015. www.nytimes.com/2015/05/03/business/pension-funds-can-only-guess-at-private-equitys-cost.html?_r=0.

Mullin, Emily. "How to Pay for Nursing Home Costs." *US News & World Report*. http://health.usnews.com/health-news/best-nursing-homes/articles/2013/02/26/how-to-pay-for-nursing-home-costs.

National Center for Health Statistics. http://www.cdc.gov/nchs.

Pfeiffer, Joseph C. and Christine Lazaro. *Major Investor Losses Due to Conflicted Advice: Brokerage Industry Advertising Creates the Illusion of a Fiduciary Duty: Misleading Ads Fuel Confusion, Underscore Need for Fiduciary Standard*. Public Investors Arbitration Bar Association Report. March 25, 2015. https://piaba.org/system/files/pdfs/PIABA%20Conflicted%20Advice%20Report.pdf.

Phillips, Steven R. and Betsy Wackernagle Bach. "The Metaphors of Retirement: Cutting Cords, Disentangling from Webs, and Heading for Pasture." University of Montana Scholar Works. scholarworks.umt.edu/cgi/viewcontent.cgi?article=1006&context=communications_pubs.

Powell, Robert. "Five Strategies to Get the Most Social Security." MarketWatch. March 29, 2014. www.marketwatch.com/story/five-strategies-to-get-the-most-social-security-2014-03-15.

Robert Powell. "You may need less retirement income than you think." MarketWatch. December 24, 2015. http://www.marketwatch.com/story/you-may-need-less-retirement-income-than-you-think-2015-11-30.

President Barack Obama. "Remarks by the President at White House Conference on Aging." Speech. The White House. July 13, 2015. www.whitehouse.gov/the-press-office/2015/07/13/remarks-president-white-house-conference-aging.

Prial, Dunstan. "Huge Wall Street Fines Raise Calls for More Transparency." Fox Business. June 13, 2013. http://www.foxbusiness.com/politics/2014/06/13/huge-wall-street-fines-raise-calls-for-more-transparency-1287760936.html.

"Public Pensions Watch 2015." Actuarial Outpost. http://www. actuarialoutpost.com/actuarial_discussion_forum/showthread. php?t=288895.

Racioppi, Dustin. "Some State Pensions in Dire Straits." *USA Today.* March 21, 2014. www.usatoday.com/story/news/nation/2014/03/21/ public-pensions-in-perilous-straits/6684383.

Regnier, Pat. "Jack Bogle Explains How the Index Fund Won with Investors." *Money.* July 27, 2015. http://time.com/money/3956351/ jack-bogle-index-fund.

Reisner, Rebecca. "How the Rule of 72 Can Help You Build Up Your Retirement Nest Egg." *Forbes Personal Finance.* January 14, 2016.

"Retirement Confidence Survey." Employee Benefit Research Institute. https://www.ebri.org/surveys/rcs.

Roberts, Kenneth. "Junk Bonds Turn Up the Risk for Retirees." MarketWatch. May 29, 2014. www.marketwatch.com/story/ junk-bonds-turn-up-the-risk-for-retirees-2014-05-29.

Rosato, Donna. "Workers Spend More Time Researching Cars Than Checking Out 401(k) Options." *Money.* August 21, 2014, time.com/ money/3149407/401k-research-spend-less-time-than-buying-cars.

Rosenbaum, Eric. "What Even Vanguard and Fidelity Can't Figure Out." CNBC. November 4, 2013. www.cnbc.com/2013/11/04/what-even-vanguard-and-fidelity-cant-figure-out.html.

"Schwab Survey Finds Workers Highly Value Their 401(k) but Are More Likely to Get Help Changing Their Oil Than Managing Their Investments." Charles Schwab. August 14, 2014. http://pressroom.aboutschwab.com/ press-release/schwab-corporate-retirement-services-news/ schwab-survey-finds-workers-highly-value-the.

Scism, Leslie. "Long-Term-Care Insurance: Is It Worth It?" *Wall Street Journal.* May 1, 2015. www.wsj.com/articles/ long-term-care-insurance-is-it-worth-it-1430488733.

"7 Mutual Fund Ads You'll Never See." MarketWatch. June 19, 2013. http://www.marketwatch.com/ story/7-mutual-fund-ads-youll-never-see-2013-06-19.

Sheehy, Kelsey. "Want a Healthy Rich Retirement? Keep Working." *USA Today.* June 6, 2015. www.usatoday. com/story/money/personalfinance/2015/06/06/ nerdwallet-working-in-retirement/28435685/.

Sightings, Tom. "How to Reboot Your Retirement." *Money.* May 4, 2015. money.usnews.com/money/blogs/on-retirement/2015/05/04/ how-to-reboot-your-retirement.

Sisti, George. "It's OK. Live a Little in Retirement." MarketWatch. May 29, 2015, www.marketwatch.com/story/ its-ok-live-a-little-in-retirement-2015-05-29.

Skinner, Liz. "Brokers Get a Mixed Review on How They Treat Older Investors." *Investmenat News.* April 15, 2015.

Social Security Administration. "When to Start Receiving Retirement Benefits." www.ssa.gov/pubs/EN-05-10147.pdf.

Sommer, Jeff. "Give Fees an Inch, and They'll Take a Mile." *New York Times.* March 1, 2014.

Spiegelman, Rande. "When Should You Take Social Security?" Charles Schwab. June 1, 2015. www.schwab.com/public/schwab/nn/articles/ When-Should-You-Take-Social-Security.

Stern, Corey. "Baby Boomers Own Too Much Stock." *Business Insider.* July 30, 2015.

Steverman, Ben. "Five Ways Your Financial Adviser Can Screw Up Your Retirement, Legally." *Bloomberg Business.* February 23, 2015.

"Supporting Retirement for American Families." Executive Office of the President Council of Economic Advisers. February 2, 2012. www.whitehouse. gov/sites/default/files/cea_retirement_report_01312012_final.pdf.

The Time Has Come for Standardized Total Cost Disclosure for Private Equity. CEM Benchmarking. April 2015. http://www.cembenchmarking.com/Files/Documents/CEM_article_-_The_time_has_come_for_standardized_total_cost_disclosure_for_private_equity.pdf.

Tuchman, Mitch. "Why 99% of Trading Is Pointless." *MoneyWatch*. August 1, 2015. http://www.marketwatch.com/story/why-99-of-trading-is-pointless-john-bogle-2015-07-30.

Tuohy, Cyril. "Even 'Relatively Sophisticated' Investors Need Help from Advisors." Insurance News Net. May 2015.

US Census Bureau. http://www.census.gov.

US National Library of Medicine. ihm.nlm.nih.gov/luna/servlet/detail/NLMNLM~1~1~101435627~139833:-Medical-instruments-and-apparatus-.

"Variable Annuities: What You Should Know." US Securities and Exchange Commission. www.sec.gov/investor/pubs/varannty.htm.

Study on Investment Advisers and Broker-Dealers. US Securities and Exchange Commission. January 2011.

Veres, Bob. "The Case against Wall Street." Advisor Perspectives. December 22, 2015. http://www.advisorperspectives.com/articles/2015/12/22/the-case-against-wall-street.

Vernon, Steve. "Do We Really Have a Retirement Crisis?" CBS. July 31, 2015. www.cbsnews.com/news/do-we-really-have-a-retirement-crisis.

Vernon, Steve. "The Biggest Retirement Planning Mistake of All." MoneyWatch. September 27, 2012. www.cbsnews.com/news/the-biggest-retirement-planning-mistake-of-all.

Viesturs, Ed. *No Shortcuts to the Top* (New York, Broadway Books, 2006).

Waggoner, John. "Investing: Lessons from 14 Years of Misery." *USA Today*. March 13, 2014.

Waggoner, John. "The Horror of Mutual Fund Taxes." *USA Today.* October 31, 2013.

"Why 99% of Trading is Pointless." MarketWatch. August 1, 2015. www.marketwatch.com/story/ why-99-of-trading-is-pointless-john-bogle-2015-07-30.

Woellert, Lorraine. "Twinkies Bankruptcy Exposes Peril to Some U.S. Pensions." *Bloomberg Business.* February 26, 2014. www.bloomberg.com/news/articles/2014-02-26/ twinkies-bankruptcy-raises-specter-of-u-s-pension-fund-failures.

"Working with a Financial Advisor Doubles Retirement Preparedness: John Hancock Retirement Plan Services Survey." John Hancock. January 21, 2016. http://www.johnhancock.com/about/news_details. php?fn=jan2116-text&yr=2016.

"Worst funded corporate pension plans." Pensions & Investments. April 30, 2013. http://www.pionline.com/gallery/20130430/ SLIDESHOW2/430009998/1.

"2012 Retirement Confidence Survey." Employee Benefit Research Institute. 2012. https://www.ebri.org/surveys/rcs/2012.